A Backward Look at Traveled Roads

Robert M. Kurtz Jr.

Also by Robert M. Kurtz, Jr.:

Kurtz Bros.: A Centennial History, 1894-1994

Future Passages: Icons Your Children May Never Know
Historic Photographs of Central Pennsylvania

Thomas Betts of Guilford and His Descendants (1615-2001)
(in collaboration with William W. Betts, III)

Americana Roads

Library of Congress Control Number: 2009910924

ISBN 0-9665451-2-5

Published by Robert M. Kurtz, Jr., Clearfield, Pennsylvania

Designed by Murphy/Carpenter, State College, Pennsylvania

Printed by Jostens Commercial Printing Services,
State College, Pennsylvania

Printed in the U.S.A.

To Marilyn

With love and affection, for those many
roads we've traveled together...

And to our grandchildren:

Colin, Karis, Robby, Sam, Sophie,
Garrett, Wyatt, Helena and their cousins,
Colin, Ryan and Adam

Introduction

*T*hose who have enjoyed Rob Kurtz's first two volumes of photographs can now anticipate with much excitement the appearance of a third album. In *Future Passages* he documented with his beautiful photographs the central portion of his native Pennsylvania. These regional images feature quaint country churches, rural delivery mailboxes, old-style milk cans, covered bridges, Amish buggies, and antique hotels. Here too are striking scenes of nature's wonder: the brilliant wildflowers, the giant moths, the Susquehanna River's West Branch, mushrooms, the white-tailed deer, stately groves of birches.

In *Americana Roads*, Kurtz ventured out from central Pennsylvania into the fifty states of the nation, organizing photographs into geographic

sections. Here are the one-room country schoolhouse, church cemeteries, Indian ruins, weathered old barns, and, again, unforgettably beautiful natural scenes, like a Teton meadow in Wyoming, the pueblo ruins of New Mexico, the Santee River Delta of South Carolina, the farm windmills of Kansas, delicate ferns in a cathedral of pines, and spectacular views of mountain lakes and inspiring landscapes.

Now in *A Backward Look at Traveled Roads* appear more of the same. Well, more of the same but with a difference.

The real subject of the first two volumes is the character of America. The photographs provide a moving history, an instructive account of the birth and growth of a nation, a visual record of the qualities that produced the country that we have become. One views many of the images with a striking sense of self-reliance, of energy, of respect for one's neighbor, of delight in children, of a faith in a supreme power, and of a reverence for the natural world.

Not surprisingly, Kurtz's world is an agrarian one. It is a world that is fast vanishing, and for him there is emotion and pain in that. It is the land that inspires him. It is the world of Willa Cather and Sarah Orne Jewett, Robert Frost and Henry Thoreau and John Muir, Grant Wood and Andrew Wyeth, of Grandma Moses, and the world of photographers, Walker Evans and Dorothea Lange. The scenes are of a time to be relished, of milking by hand, of tapping the sugar maples, of plowing with horses, of the butter churn, the oil lamp and the quill pen.

This is nostalgia. But it is not that Kurtz urges a return to the "good old days." It's the *character* of those days that he would clearly like to see sustained. There is no photograph in his work which is not in tune with this theme.

In this third volume he extends his horizons. Rob Kurtz grew up in the small community of Clearfield, Pennsylvania, which some 220 years ago was the site of the seventeenth-century Delaware Indian village known as Chinklacamoose. He enjoyed his early life on the

West Branch of the meandering Susquehanna River, somewhat remote from the big world. But he soon became a world traveler. And, naturally, for his many excursions his camera served as guide. In *A Backward Look* he shares his experiences with the reader. Here are many photographs of Old England and the British Isles, which, Kurtz believes, provided the chief ingredient for the melting pot that was to become America.

Here are Stonehenge, Hadrian's Wall, Tintern Abbey, Wordsworth's cottage in the Lake District, Runnymede, Stoke Poges, Canterbury, Thomas Hardy's cottage, views of the moors and stunning photographs of beautiful English gardens. But it is not only England, Scotland and Wales. We are transported also to exotic corners of the wide world, to Papua, New Guinea, to the Serengeti Plain, to Easter Island, to Timbuktu, to Cambodia, to the Galapagos Islands, to Morocco, and of course the Taj Mahal. Even to southern France and Roman ruins.

And there is another difference. As in the first two volumes, we have the rural United States (Pennsylvania, New England, the Prairie States, the South, the Southwest, and the Far West), and while his subject remains America, or the stuff that made America, here in this volume appears a more direct concern for history. Kurtz is a history buff – as his preface to *Americana Roads* will resoundingly testify. In *A Backward Look,* for both England and America, are scenes from battles fought, as at Hastings or Lexington-Concord, or during the Civil War. Here are the Springfield home of President Lincoln, the birthplaces of John Adams and Calvin Coolidge and the home of Carl Sandburg. Also appearing are photographs of a Shaker Village and the Old North Church in Boston.

As in the first two volumes, the photographs of *A Backward Look* are incredibly beautiful. Indeed, it is best to think of them as paintings. Against the frightening spill of the years, like a poem or a painting, a Kurtz photograph arrests for all time a precious moment of a past time. And, like poems and paintings, the photographs awaken sensations. Each inspires a mood, excites a feeling. Kurtz has insisted that a photograph enables people to see beyond what their vision allows. I know what he means. For me, a great photograph, like these we have from Kurtz, has transporting power. A photograph of the Antietam battlefield can take me there, can walk me over the Bloody Angle, and evoke in me a great sense of sadness, as many works of art can often do. And a photograph of the wagon wheels and ruts worn from the "prairie schooners" can carry me west, I might say wistfully, with the homesteaders. It is the wash of history, if you will.

Kurtz is a master photographer. His gifts are many. He clearly appreciates the value of evening light. And he can work with light to accentuate, or play down, tones and shades and colors. He knows how to compose a photograph and will labor hard to get it "just right." With angles he can make prominent a seemingly insignificant detail in such a way as to render the subject meaningful and memorable. But it's not so much his mechanics and technique that constitute his strength. It's his intuition. He can sense what it is that provides aesthetic pleasure. His art owes much to his capacity to perceive the emotional value of a scene.

His photographs are in the tradition of the work done by Walker Evans and Dorothea Lange and Ken Scott, to whose *Michigan's Leelanau County* he was introduced by his wife Marilyn, his faithful and most helpful companion on nearly all the photograph expeditions.

Kurtz has taken thousands of photos. In selecting from them for each of the three volumes he of course experienced problems. We cannot quarrel with his choices. We might only wish that we could have them all.

Naturally, many of his photos have appeared elsewhere, as, for instance,

his exceptional images of the headquarters of both Washington and Lafayette at the Brandywine battlefield, and the soldiers' huts at Valley Forge. Many of these photographs have been on exhibit and published in magazines, the largest exhibit being at the Museum of Fine Arts in Hagerstown, Maryland, with another exhibit at The Mercersburg Academy's Burgin Center for the Arts in Mercersburg, Pennsylvania.

So many are the photographs and so impressive are they that it might seem Kurtz is taking his viewer here, there and everywhere, the conductor of a hodgepodge. But, in fact, two themes dominate his work. As noted already, there is, first the plaintive lament for a way of life that is vanishing, the rural life of hard work, self-sufficiency and intimacy with the land; second, there is the celebration of a natural beauty that is being fast crowded out by a burgeoning population and the relentless growth of cities.

These are coffee-table books. They belong conspicuous in the sitting room, or on the veranda or patio. These volumes afford great pleasure and deserve to be enjoyed over and over, by all members of the family or guests in the home. Needless to note, the photographs are so absorb-

ing that almost every one promptly becomes a favorite. A mountain stream, a chipmunk with a strawberry, an Amish horse and carriage, an Indian grinding stone, a desert monument, the Concord bridge, the earthworks at Yorktown. And it is with great confidence that I invite you to that same sense of privilege. Here for your continuing enjoyment are the 300 photographs of *A Backward Look at Traveled Roads.*

William W. Betts, III,
Indiana University of Pennsylvania,
English Professor Emeritus

The boast of heraldry, the pomp of pow'r,
And all that beauty, all that wealth e'er gave,
Awaits alike th' inevitable hour:
The paths of glory lead but to the grave.

Elegy Written in a Country Churchyard
- Thomas Gray

X

Preface

This, the third book in my trilogy of three historical photo-documentary books, is geographically the most encompassing. The first book, *Future Passages*, dealt exclusively with central Pennsylvania; it was followed by *Americana Roads*, which covered the continental United States. This third volume encompasses the world, yet it, too, returns to central Pennsylvania and the theme of my first two books as well as the place of my roots and those of a large number of my readers.

Those of you who know me, or have read my other books, know that my heart lies in the rural, off-the-beaten track areas of our land. I seek to travel far from the Interstate highways, seeking out the solitude of small towns, back roads and scenic byways, hoping to find

the quieter, unspoiled and gentle world of common folk and how their uneventful lives and material environment, woven together with those of millions of others, have contributed to the greatness of this nation.

Each artist reflects his own time, space and emotions in his or her writings, paintings and photography. I have been impressed by those of America's best artists who have depicted the character of America through familiar and ordinary scenes that have become icons of our past. Artists such as Edward Hopper, Andrew Wyeth, Grant Wood and writers in the vein of Mark Twain, Willa Cather and Sarah Orne Jewett, along with photographers

Walker Evans, Dorothea Lange and Wright Morris stand out. Each depicts a distinctly American spirit of time, loneliness and space.

In their own way, these artists and writers often portray nostalgic scenes of deserted buildings or lonely landscapes which act as surrogates for the human presence or emotions recalled from the past. The emptiness of a brooding landscape or a sense of quiet loneliness is evoked in their works. A search for similar scenes, and the character and values they portray, has led me to explore many rural and less populated sections of America.

I seek to highlight some little known but significant historic places, always keeping in mind that those who lived in a time past can never see events with the clarity we do, for they did not know the future, just as we have difficulty putting into perspective those events that take place during our time. The future will read our time differently from how we view it today. My photographs seek to preserve our time and to show those in the future how the present looks to those of us living now.

I try to portray the land and how it has shaped what man has done in living *with* the land, its past, and the people who have lived there, not what man has done *to* the land, in the sense of bulldozing highways, the building of dams, cities and other massive infrastructure, all done for man's benefit, but often destroying the natural beauty and even historical relevance and a way of life, for his own purposes.

Historic sights are often more authentic when left without elaborate visitors centers or other improvements which so often are done in the name of better access for bringing history to more people, progress, however, for which we pay a price. Unless done with a concern for permitting the historical relevance of the site to dominate our more recent interpretations, which can never be the same as held by those who lived at that time, we often have difficulty understanding the historical events which led to the particular site and how those events impacted the history that followed. "Site sanctification," as historians call it, begins with denoting a simple historical event to which we increasingly add ever more irrelevant non-historic "improvements" such as statues and monuments, fences, towers, paved roads, tourist lodgings and attractions, visitors centers and all that goes with them, including key chains, coffee mugs, ball caps, tee shirts and the like. When done with taste, putting history first, the results can be rewarding. However, too often the improvements result in what the *National Geographic Traveler* magazine refers to as the shopping mall atmosphere, as for example, at the Mt. Rushmore National Monument site or the artificial and unnatural skywalk at the Grand Canyon. These are but two examples. Unfortunately, others abound.

Since this may be my last book, I have felt less inhibited about including a few personal and family references that were previously avoided. I hope this does not detract from the reflection of historical lore; perhaps it may even contribute to that effect.

Those of us who live on either of the two continental coasts, and that includes most of us, are often immunized from the great heartland between. We jump on a plane on one coast, and fly across the continent to alight on the other coast, acquiring little knowledge of the land or its people between.

If we take the time to look at the land we're flying over, often an education in itself, we can appreciate those squared off tracks of land, especially in the Midwest, bounded by roads which often mark the 160 acres granted to the homesteaders. Or perhaps we can marvel at the vast uninhabited land of rural areas and rivers that played such a critical role in the movement westward, or the prairies and deserts that had to be traversed by wagon or on foot. Sometimes we glimpse a striking view of golden wheat fields or majestic snowcapped mountains. It's interesting to watch the shadows of cloud formations projected on the

ground in the shape of the very clouds over which we are passing.

On any flight, I often study the towns below, my thoughts occupied by how they compare with Willa Cather's Red Cloud, or her fictionalized villages of the Black Hawk of Jim Burden and Antonia, the Sweet Water of *A Lost Lady* or the Haverford of *Lucy Gayhart*, or perhaps Grover's Corners in Thorton Wilder's play *Our Town* or my own town of Clearfield, Pennsylvania. I see them not as provincial towns, as some would cynically portray them, but rather in the context of thousands of different neighborhoods with individual cultures, dreams and aspirations, comprising the cities and towns, large and small, that span this continent, and that are America.

Each town or city has its own distinct social strata. Even our largest cities have their smugness and provincialism, no matter how much the inhabitants may protest otherwise. Sinclair Lewis' *Main Street* is America's Main Street, whether it is his Gopher Prairie, Minnesota or New York City. Only the individuals and their cultural and political orientations and prejudices differ; all have their own recognizable brand of provincialism, otherwise called enlightenment, which too often looks with disdain on those of different orientations or persuasions.

Robert M. Kurtz Jr.

Clearfield, Pennsylvania
July 20, 2009

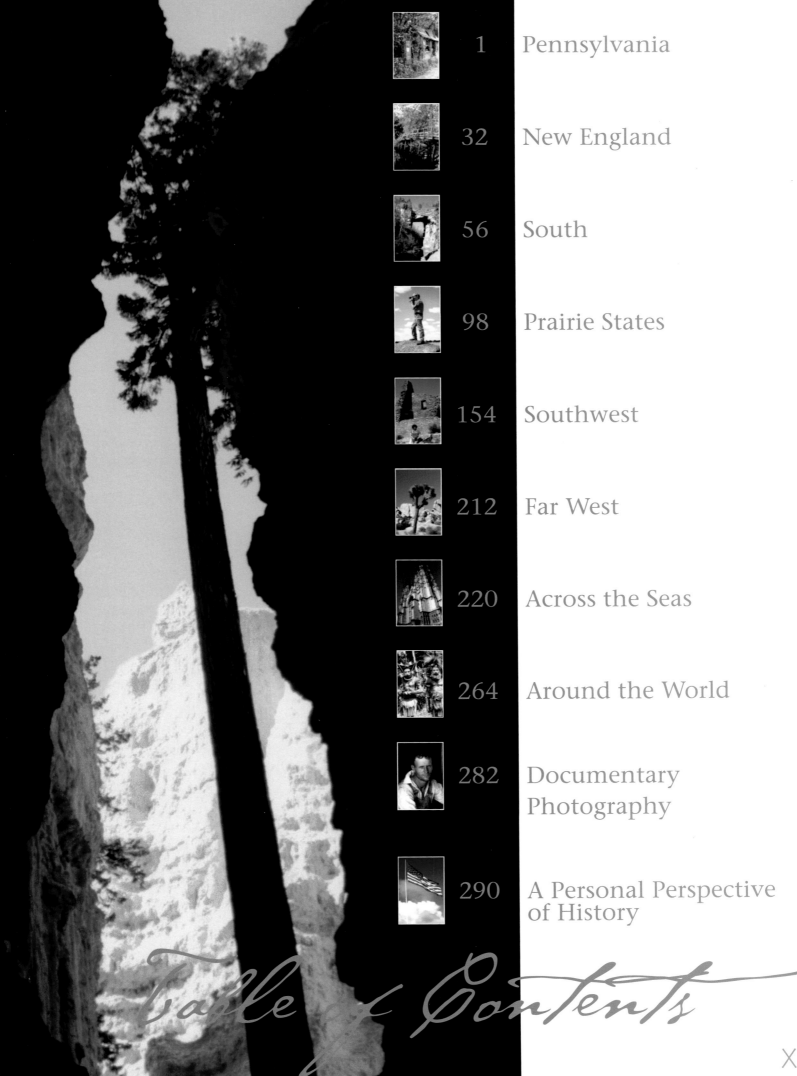

Table of Contents

XIII

A Backward Look at Traveled Roads

Roadside Sentinel

This gas pump registers twenty-nine cents per gallon.

Route 26, south of Saxton, Pennsylvania

ATLANTIC

Pennsylvania

Amish Hay Wagon and Horses
Near Smicksburg, Pennsylvania

Pennsylvania

Amish Barn Raising

Built using the ancient Amish timber-frame technique, which does not require nails, this barn was raised at the Cooke Tavern Bed & Breakfast in Penn Hall, near Spring Mills. This central Pennsylvania valley, east of State College, is home to many Amish farmers.

Route 45. Pennsylvania

3

1830 Barn

Placed in the Centre County Farmland Trust by Hugh and Barbara Hodge, this barn, with massive internal beams as long as 90 feet, was built in 1830. It is decorated with hand carved artwork. Farmland Trusts plays an important role in preserving the green spaces surrounding many urban developments.

Penn Township, Centre County, Pennsylvania

Pennsylvania

Abandoned Farmhouse

This house evokes memories of what many farmhouses once were like.

Burnt Cabins, Pennsylvania

The Great Circus Train Wreck

It was early on the morning of May 30, 1893, that the Walter L. Main circus, after successful performances in Houtzdale, Pennsylvania, was being carried on the Tyrone & Clearfield branch of the Pennsylvania Railroad to its next destination at Lewistown. One of the largest circuses of that time, it required seventeen railcars. Because of excessive speed the train derailed at a sharp curve known as McCann's Crossing. In the ensuing wreck, six circus personnel were killed and a dozen badly injured. All the animals, including elephants, zebras, tigers, lions, horses, monkeys, birds, and snakes escaped. Only a few were recaptured. The show, however, recovered and continued in many forms until 1937. Even to this day, more than 116 years later, circus performers, both retired and active, including many loyal local circus fans, still gather annually to commemorate the memory of that fateful circus disaster.

East of Tyrone, Village of Olivia,
off Route 220 on Vanscoyoc Hollow Road

Great Clearfield Fire and John Robinson Circus

The John Robinson Circus was playing in Clearfield on Sunday afternoon, July 24, 1881, when the town's premier hotel, The Shaw House, located on Front Street, caught fire. Initially it was feared that the entire business portion of the town would be destroyed. With the river only a block away, a bucket brigade with water buckets passed hand to hand was quickly formed. Even small boys, who received special mention for their efforts, were pressed into service. Men were stationed on the roofs of all nearby buildings. Nearly a hundred circus people and spectators assisted the local firemen. Had it not been for the help of the circus people, the entire center of Clearfield would likely have been destroyed. The fire was of such magnitude that two of the circus people died of burns. The John Robinson Circus returned to Clearfield each year, through the early 1920s, to perform and place flowers on the graves in memory of the heroic circus people who helped save the town of Clearfield. Such is the loyalty and devotion of circus personnel. "That circus has not been forgotten. To this day, the story is told to the great-grandchildren of the townspeople of Clearfield," said Dorothy Betts Kurtz in a story she wrote of the fire, taken from oral history, which was published in *Good Old Days* magazine.

Pennsylvania

Bucktails

This Civil War Memorial commemorates the highly esteemed Company K of the Bucktail Regiment, commanded by Captain Edward A. Irvin. The Regiment fought many battles, including Gettysburg, Antietam and South Mountain. In front of the Civil War Memorial is a statute of an American World War I soldier, or Doughboy, the nickname given to WW I American soldiers.

On May 8, 1861, Jane Irwin, mother of Captain Irvin, presented the Regimental flag, which she had designed, to Company K as it was departing from Curwensville for Camp Curtin to answer President Lincoln's call for an additional 75,000 men. That flag followed the Regiment throughout the war. After Captain Irwin was captured, Jane and her husband William played an historic role when they met with President Lincoln and urged his support for the exchange of captured Union and Confederate troops. Jane Irwin passed through the Union and Confederate battle lines three times in this endeavor. She also visited the battlefield hospitals at South Mountain and Antietam. A re-enactment of the day when she presented the flag to the regiment was held at the same spot at the Irwin home at 240 State Street, 138 years later, on May 8, 1999. The blood-stained flag survived the war, but became lost during the ensuing years.

Curwensville, Pennsylvania

Bloody Knox

This 1860s cabin was the site of a bloody Civil War shootout between draft dodgers and Union troops. Nearly 450 draft dodgers and deserters were working in the area as loggers, while also looting throughout the county. Secret societies were formed to resist the draft and gather slaves. Former Governor William Bigler, who was anti-Lincoln, lived in the area and was sympathetic to these woodsmen. On December 13, 1864, one deserter, Tom Adams, owner of the cabin, and one Union soldier were killed here. Later, more than 150 men were incarcerated. Only New York City suffered more civil disobedience and violence during the war, which ended four months later, than did Clearfield County.

Route 453 north of Madera, Pennsylvania

Rain Barrel at Bloody Knox

Pennsylvania

Mail Pouch Barn

Mail Pouch barns scattered on rural roads throughout Pennsylvania have always been a popular photographic subject. These barns were painted as advertisements for the Mail Pouch Tobacco Company, Wheeling, West Virginia, from 1890 to 1992. A desire to capture these barns for posterity, combined with a desire to photograph backyard wildlife with encouragement from Marilyn, led to my serious photography.

Route 522, south of Shirleysburg, Pennsylvania

Snow Fence

Although snow is absent here, these fences, while seldom seen today, were once commonly used to prevent blowing snow from drifting across rural roads, which often lacked snow removal equipment.

Pennsylvania

Zion Union Cemetery

After President Lincoln issued the Emancipation Proclamation in January 1863, which permitted African Americans to serve in the Union army, 88 blacks from Mercersburg enlisted in the army. They were assigned to the Massachusetts 54th Regiment. At that time Mercersburg, just north of the Mason-Dixon Line, was the largest free black community in the country. Of those who enlisted, one quarter had been slaves.

This black cemetery is the largest burial ground of the Massachusetts 54th Regiment of African American Civil War veterans.

Still undergoing study is the important role played by Mercersburg in the Underground Railroad, which smuggled slaves north of the Mason-Dixon Line to freedom.

Bennett Avenue, Mercersburg, Pennsylvania

Pennsylvania Corn Harvest

Pennsylvania

Fall Barn Scene

Saint Marys Covered Bridge
Route 522, south of Orbisonia, Pennsylvania

Pennsylvania

Fulton House Stagecoach Stop

Built in 1793, this stone building was an early stagecoach stop, tavern and boardinghouse. A pioneer cabin, built in 1783, is in the rear.

McConnellsburg, Pennsylvania

General Hugh Mercer Springhouse

Pictured above is the remaining part of the Hugh Mercer stone springhouse.
At that time Mercer was a physician on what was then the frontier. The town
and the present-day Academy, a coeducational boarding school, were named
in his honor. He died during the Revolutionary War Battle of Princeton, which
followed Washington's December 25 Crossing of the Delaware River in 1776.
Mercer had settled here shortly after emigrating from Scotland in 1746.

This area of Pennsylvania, which at the time was the western frontier, played
an important role in the French and Indian War (1753-1763), also called
The Seven Years' War, which preceded the Revolution. The Conococheague
Institute, complete with reconstructed buildings and a large library, located
a few miles outside of Mercersburg, preserves much of this early history.

Off Route 16 on Hissong Road, east of Mercersburg, Pennsylvania

Pennsylvania

Witherspoon Covered Bridge

Built in 1883 this 87-foot long covered bridge over Licking Creek features a Burr arch-truss, vertical plank siding and a gable roof.

Off route 16 on Anderson Road, west of Greencastle, Pennsylvania

"Crown Stone" Mason-Dixon Marker

The traditional dividing line between North and South, the Mason-Dixon Line, was surveyed by Charles Mason and Jeremiah Dixon in 1760 to settle a dispute over lands claimed by Pennsylvania on the north and Maryland on the south. Stone markers were placed every mile, with "Crown Markers," those bearing the coat of arms of the Penn and Calvert families, placed at each five-mile point along the survey line. Above is one of the few remaining "Crown Markers."

For enslaved African-Americans escaping from the South on the Underground Railroad, crossing the Mason-Dixon Line was the goal of their freedom trek north. Many settled just a few miles north of this line in Mercersburg, which at that time harbored the largest free black settlement in the United States.

Route 163, one and a half miles west of the Pennsylvania town of State Line, in the backyard of a farmhouse

Pennsylvania

Price's Mill Bridge

This five-arch stone bridge was built in 1822 over the Conococheague Creek just south of the Mason-Dixon Line. This bridge was placed over a natural ford in the creek, the logical place for wagons to cross and a mill to be built. In June 1863 Confederate troops probably crossed this bridge on their way to Gettysburg and the burning of Chambersburg.

Off Maryland Route 58, on a private farm south of Mercersburg Pennsylvania

Small Stone Arch Bridge

Confederate troops passed this way while marching through southern Pennsylvania toward Chambersburg, which they burned before going on to the Battle of Gettysburg.

Route 416 south of Mercersburg, Pennsylvania

Pennsylvania

Red Maple and Sergeant (Weeping) Hemlock

Founders Hall

In February 1989, ten community leaders of Clearfield had the vision of establishing a college for higher education, with special emphasis on local and non-traditional students of the immediate area. These men, David A. Bailey, Carl A. Belin, Jr., William L. Bertram, Guy A. Graham, William E. Johnston, Robert M. Kurtz, Jr., James P. Moore, Stanley Rakowsky, Peter F. Smith and William K. Ulerich joined together to provide the necessary means for Lock Haven University to establish a branch campus in Clearfield.

This campus area formerly was part of the Goldenrod Dairy Farm owned by Charles T. Kurtz. The farm had been noted for record potato harvests. Presently the area of the farm, in addition to the college campus, is the site of the Goldenrod and Rivers Bend residential developments. Enrollment at the University is currently approximately 500 students.

Clearfield Campus, Lock Haven University

Pennsylvania

Dimeling Hotel

Built in 1904 by Beezer Brothers Architects and Builders of Pittsburgh, this landmark in downtown Clearfield is on the National Register of Historic Places.

Second and Market Streets, Clearfield

Antique Farm Tractor
Route 522 south of Mount Union, Pennsylvania

Farm Truck
Route 522 south of Mount Union, Pennsylvania

Pennsylvania

Antique Red Truck
*Route 522 south of Shirleysburg,
Pennsylvania*

Shade Gap Presbyterian Church

The congregation of this church dates back to 1799. The church was built in 1848. The adjoining church cemetery includes several Revolutionary War graves.

Route 522, Shade Gap, Pennsylvania

Pennsylvania

Drake Oil Well

It seems strange to realize that the world's first oil was drilled on August 27, 1859, in northwestern Pennsylvania. Edwin Drake had gone there to develop a method to improve the output from an oil spring in the ground. When all other means failed, he devised a drill derrick enclosed in an engine house which penetrated the ground around the spring. It was so successful that thousands of wells and derricks promptly sprang up in the nearby area, resulting in so much oil being produced that the price plummeted so low that Drake and his partners soon went out of business.

Route 8 Titusville, Pennsylvania

Confederate Soldiers

In what were the first Confederate Civil War deaths on Pennsylvania soil north of the Mason-Dixon Line, these two Confederate soldiers were killed on June 30, 1863, in a skirmish with local citizens.

Route 16, east of McConnellsburg, Pennsylvania

Pennsylvania

Three Confederate Soldiers

In the aftermath of the Gettysburg Battle, many wounded soldiers found their way to towns along the Pennsylvania-Maryland border. One of these towns was Mercersburg, Pennsylvania, which in addition to having the largest population of free blacks in the north also played a significant role in the Underground Railroad. Several of the present-day Academy buildings were used as hospitals for the wounded. Both Union and Confederate soldiers were treated equally. Three of the Confederates were so badly wounded that they died and were buried side by side in the Fairview Cemetery.

Two of these three were named, with the third grave marked as "Unknown." Forty years later one of the Academy teachers, Archibald Rutledge, who had lived in the South, wrote an article for the *Richmond Times-Dispatch* newspaper, naming the two known soldiers: J. W. Alban and W. H. Quaintance.

Shortly thereafter, a letter arrived from a Hallie Quaintance, stating that she was sure that the young soldier she had married many years ago as a young bride was the Will Quaintance in the cemetery, who in his last parting breaths kept calling out for "Hallie." She only knew that he had fought at Gettysburg, but had never heard from him again. By pure chance she read the newspaper article written by Rutledge. After forty years she had finally found her husband! In a community ceremony held for her, many surviving Union veterans welcomed her into their hearts.

Mercersburg, Pennsylvania

Harriet Lane House

The Lane House was built by Thomas C. Lane in 1830. It was here that Harriet Lane was born. She was a niece to James Buchanan (1791-1861), 15th President of the United States. Since Buchanan was a bachelor, Harriet was the official mistress at the White House. Buchanan was born just a few miles outside of Mercersburg.

14 North Main Street, Mercersburg, Pennsylvania

Pennsylvania

Sophie

The Halloween wicked
witch at age three

Backyard Grey Fox

Autumn Color at a New England Pond
New Hampshire

New England

New England Stone Walls
New Hampshire

New England

Henry Whitfield House

Built in 1639, this is the oldest house in Connecticut and the oldest stone house in New England. At that time Thomas Betts (of my family ancestry), who came to this country from England and was one of the original settlers and founders of Guilford, owned land adjoining the Whitfield house. Along with Reverend Henry Whitfield, Betts and others laid out the town and negotiated the purchase of land from the Indians on September 29, 1639.

Guilford, Connecticut

Grange Hall
Grafton, Vermont

New England

House Barn

Barns such as this, built as part of a house, seem to be unique to New England.
Maine

New England

The Howland House
Westport Harbor, Massachusetts

Meeting House

This meeting house was raised the day of the Battle of Lexington – Concord, which was the first battle of the Revolutionary War, April 19, 1775. The writer Willa Cather (1873-1947) spent many summers in this town. She is buried in the adjacent cemetery. Her headstone is engraved with a quotation from her novel *My Antonia*: *"That is happiness: to be dissolved into something complete and great."*

Jaffrey Center, New Hampshire

New England

Little Compton Cemetery

Here is a marker for Captain Owen Wilbour, 66 years of age, lost at sea on August 23, 1853, and his son, young Wilbour, aged 20, also lost at sea on July 2, 1851, two years earlier.

Little Compton, Rhode Island

"You recall the graveyard and the old story writing

itself over and over? Only it is we who write it,

with the best we have."

O Pioneers!

-Willa Cather

Sarah Orne Jewett Home

Recognized as one of the foremost American writers of the nineteenth century, Sarah Orne Jewett was best known for her novel *The Country of the Pointed Firs*. Several short stories, especially "A White Heron," "The Only Rose" and "A Bit of Shore Life," are particularly enjoyable. Although the stories may seem a bit outdated by today's standards, they give a good feel for living on the Maine coast in the late 1800s. Willa Cather called her writing "almost flawless examples of literary art." To readers her writings *are* Maine.

South Berwick, Maine

New England

The House of Seven Gables

The novel by the same name as the house, and *The Scarlet Letter*, are two of the most famous works by Nathaniel Hawthorne, one of American's greatest writers.

Salem, Massachusetts

Spire of the Old North Church

He said to his friend, "If the British march
By land or sea from the town to-night,
Hang a lantern aloft in the belfry arch
Of the North Church tower as a signal light,-
One if by land, and two if by sea;
And I on the opposite shore will be,
Ready to ride and spread the alarm
Through every Middlesex village and farm,
For the country folk to be up and to arm."

The above passage, from the famous poem by Longfellow, "The Midnight Ride of Paul Revere," tells of the North Church in Boston with its historic belfry spire where the lanterns hung for the "one if by land, two if by sea" signals given to Paul Revere waiting on the opposite shore to warn of the march by the British out of Boston to Lexington. During the ride, Revere also sought to alert John Hancock and Samuel Adams of the approaching British soldiers.

Boston, Massachusetts

New England

Steps Leading Up to the Old North Church Belfry

The signal of the lanterns was devised by the Committee of Safety on Charlestown since it was feared that it would be difficult to cross the Charles River or get over "Boston neck," once troop movements began. The sight of the two lanterns, hung in the church belfry by sexton Robert Newman, told Revere that the British were making their initial troop movement by boat. By leaving the church through a side window, Newman narrowly escaped capture. Revere began his ride at eleven o'clock to alert those along the way that the British were coming in their direction. Earlier that same evening William Dawes had left Boston and taken an alternate route to provide the same warning. Revere and Dawes were both captured in the early morning hours, but each managed to escape.

The church has been the scene of many weddings, including that of Marilyn and Rob Kurtz. Later they climbed the steep belfry steps where the lanterns, which signaled the movement of the British troops, had hung on the night of April 18, 1776. Only one of the lanterns is known to exist.

Boston, Massachusetts

Battle Road

Although the original road taken by the British on April 19, 1775, advancing from Boston to Concord, and their return retreat, has undergone many changes, this section has been restored to the original dirt and clay surface. Many encounters with the British took place along this road as the "Minute Men" chased the Redcoats back to Boston. From this beginning, the Revolutionary War was to continue for more than eight years.

Minute Man National Historical Park, Massachusetts

New England

Hartwell Tavern

The Hartwell Tavern, located along the historic Battle Road, was one of the principal stopping places for travelers to share the news of the day while making the trip from Boston to Concord.

Minute Man National Historical Park, Massachusetts

Concord Bridge

After a brief skirmish on Lexington Green, the British moved on to Concord, where at the North Bridge the first brief battle of the Revolution took place when the British sought to capture the colonists' supply of gunpowder. From this first battle on April 19, 1775, until the victory at Yorktown (the last major battle), on October 19, 1781, more than six years had elapsed and twenty-five thousand (one percent of the population) had died in the conflict.

Concord, Massachusetts

New England

Shaker Village

As required by the Shaker religion, Shakers chose to live apart, in self-contained villages. Seeking to create heaven on earth, the Shakers practiced equality of sexes and races, simplicity of life, common ownership of goods, celibacy and pacifism. In over two hundred years of devoting their "Hands to Work and Hearts to God" the Shakers created their legacy of plain but distinctive architecture, furniture, crafts, inventions and song so much renowned today. The last surviving Shaker died in 1992. The Meeting House pictured above was built in 1792.

Canterbury, New Hampshire

Fort Ticonderoga

With both England and France laying claim to North America in the 1700s, the French built fortifications to protect the waterways that served their fur trade network. The area of Lake Champlain and Lake George in upper New York State was a "no-man's-land" which became a wilderness battleground for the two European powers. The French constructed a fort named Fort Carillon, from which they could command either invasion route the British might take: down Lake Champlain or over the portage from Lake George.

The French defended the fort in 1758 but the following year withdrew. The British renamed the structure Fort Ticonderoga and held it until in a bold dawn raid, on May 10, 1775, just three weeks after the Lexington and Concord battles, Benedict Arnold with Ethan Allen and his Green Mountain Boys took the fort from the British, giving America its first victory in the Revolutionary War. Its unique star shape maximizes the fields of fire and was the ultimate defensive weapon of that era.

Ticonderoga, New York

New England

Calvin Coolidge Birthplace

The 30th President of the United States, Calvin Coolidge, served from 1923 to 1929, taking the oath of office in his nightshirt, after being awakened at midnight to be told of the assassination of President Warren G. Harding. Both of the sons of Calvin and Grace Coolidge, John and Calvin, Jr., attended The Mercersburg Academy.

A quiet, plain-spoken New Englander of great reserve and little fanfare, the humble Coolidge is now rated a better President than he once was given credit for. He said, "We draw our Presidents from the people....I came from them. I wish to be one of them again."

Plymouth Notch, Vermont

Home of John and Abigail Adams

It was to this home, built just across the road from where John had been born, that John and Abigail Adams retired after his term as the second president of the United States (1797 to 1801). At that time the nation's capital was located in Philadelphia, while awaiting the construction of Washington City, to be the nation's permanent capital. Abigail and John probably enjoyed the closest relationship known to exist between a president and his wife. Although they were separated for many years during which Adams performed his official duties, he made few decisions in which he did not consult Abigail. She died in 1818, fifteen years before John.

Quincy, Massachusett

Posterity, who will reap the blessings, will scarcely be able to conceive the hardships and sufferings of their ancestors.
- Abigail Adams

New England

Birthplace of John Adams

It was into this simple and commonplace New England saltbox home of five rooms, built in 1681, that John Adams, our second President, was born in 1735.

Adams was one of the most prolific writers of all of the Founders. There were few of his contemporaries with whom he did not feud at one time or another. His relationship with Jefferson, who was Adams' Vice-President, was especially rocky. However, in later years they carried on a unique and warm correspondence, which, while each put forth his best side for posterity, has added much to the understanding of that period of the founding. In a striking coincidence, Adams and Jefferson died on the same day, July 4, 1826, exactly fifty years after the adoption of the Declaration of Independence.

It is ironic that Jefferson wrote the Declaration only after Adams had declined to do so, recommending that Jefferson, rather than he, do the writing. What would have been the rhetoric of that historic document had Adams done the writing? Had Jefferson not used the words that he did, would the Declaration have the place in history that we now give it? That document, along with the Louisiana Purchase, was Jefferson's greatest achievement. To those two events he owes his place in history. Adams, however, felt that Jefferson had taken the words from other colonial documents, and that Jefferson was a draftsman, not a mover-and-shaker.

Quincy, Massachusetts

New England

The Olsen House

The Olsen House, built in the late 1700s, was once described by a neighbor, Betsy James, as "looming up like a weathered ship stranded on a hilltop." Betsy James, who later became Mrs. Andrew Wyeth, introduced Wyeth to Christina and Alvaro Olsen, owners of the house. Over the next three decades, a growing friendship developed between the Olsens and Wyeth. It was here that Wyeth produced his most famous painting, *Christina's World*. Weyth painted the rooms and the house many times over. For him, Christina and the Olson House were symbols of New England and Maine. Christina died there in 1968.

Wyeth confirmed that when he painted *Christina's World*, little in the painting was real. Wyeth's wife Betsy posed for the figure, and only the arms and hands were modeled by Christina herself. Wyeth eliminated many of the farm's out-buildings and distorted the space between the house and barn; the slope of the hill and the tire tracks were Wyeth's invention. None of this should detract from the painting or the powerful emotions associated with it. These facts depict the difference between the painter and the photographer.

Cushing, Maine

Natural Bridge

This 215-foot-tall natural limestone bridge was carved over the centuries by the waters of Cedar Creek. The Monacan Indians knew it as "The Bridge of God" and used it as a site of worship. U.S. Route 11 passes over the top of the arch, which is not visible from the road. George Washington surveyed the property and carved his initials, which are still visible, in the stone. Thomas Jefferson bought the bridge for 20 shillings from King George III of England.

South of Lexington, Virginia, off Interstate 81

South

Yorktown

While the Yorktown surrender of the British on October 19, 1781, is known as the end of the American Revolution, the last battle actually took place on November 10, 1782, thirteen months later, when patriots retaliated against loyalist and Indian forces by attacking a Shawnee village in present-day Ohio. The photo above shows one of the defenses (called redoubts) from the last major battle at Yorktown, which secured the independence of the United States and thus significantly altered the course of world history.

It was at No. 10 redoubt that Alexander Hamilton and his light infantry rose from their trenches and raced with fixed bayonets, storming across a quarter-mile of fields pocked and rutted from exploding shells, to surprise the defending British troops. It was after this surprise attack, and with the French fleet blocking any retreat, that General Cornwallis realized the futility of further resistance. His surrender would eventually bring an end to the long war.

South

Earthworks at Yorktown

Even after the surrender of the British at Yorktown, French forces, allied with the Americans, remained in the Yorktown area. General Washington moved most of the American troops, expecting that the war would continue, to New York, which the British still occupied

Finally, more than seven years after the signing of the Declaration of Independence, the Treaty of Paris ended the American Revolution in September of 1783. Four years later the Constitutional Convention met in the summer of 1787 in Philadelphia to begin drafting the document under which we live today.

Jamestown

On December 20, 1606, three small ships with a crew of 39, carrying 106 male passengers departed London for a four and a half month voyage across the Atlantic, arriving on May 13, 1607, to found Jamestown, the first permanent English settlement in the new world. Recent excavations and interpretations have created a new understanding of the colony. For example, it is now thought highly unlikely that Captain John Smith ever married Pocahontas, who did marry John Rolfe and went to England with him, where she died at age 21.

Reconstructed James Fort at Jamestown

Until recent excavations, it was thought that James Fort had eroded into the James River. However, recent archaeology has discovered evidence that James Fort did actually continue to exist and was not washed away by the river. Above is part of the reconstructed fort.

South

"Mud and Stud" Buildings

After first constructing a sizable fort with palisade walls, 11 to 15 feet tall, in the short time of 19 days, the settlers next turned their attention to building "mud and stud" homes similar to the one shown above. Disease, famine, and Indian attacks led to the demise of nearly half of the original settlers within the first year. Gradually, with the arrival of new settlers, tobacco, corn and other crops, including trade with some of the friendly Indians, helped the colony of Jamestown to survive.

Colonial Williamsburg

It was in this room in the capital of Virginia that the House of Burgesses, meeting on May 15, 1776, gave the first serious consideration to a resolution that would take the radical and daring step of declaring full and complete independence of the colonies from England. With the adoption of that resolution, the House of Burgesses instructed their delegates to the Continental Congress to place a similar motion before that Congress. Richard Henry Lee of the Virginia delegation made that motion on June 7, 1776, at the meeting in Philadelphia. The passage of that motion by the Continental Congress led to the drafting of the Declaration of Independence and its acceptance less than a month later.

South

Williamsburg Capital Building

This reconstruction of the first capital in Williamsburg, is an example of an architectural design devised for a specific purpose. The "H" shaped building, with its two rounded main parts, housed the two legislative bodies of the General Assembly known as the House of Burgesses and the Council or the upper body of the legislature, each in one of the two separate wings. The shape of the building, not unlike the nation's capital in Washington, aided the process of mediation between the two legislative bodies.

Mt. Gilead Church

The Mt. Gilead Church was designed by architect Louis Frederick Stutz in 1896 for the congregation of what was then the Grace Lutheran Church, since moved to 16th and R Streets.

The design of the church, now the Mt. Gilead Baptist Church, reflects the elements of Gothic Revival. Its predominant architecture features rusticated stone, simple column forms supporting rounded arches and a single tower, massive and bold in outline. These are the defining elements of Richardsonian Romanesque architecture, named for American architect Henry Hobson Richardson (1838-1886), a style much admired and adopted by architects of the late 19th century for schools, post offices, commercial and federal buildings.

This church design came naturally to Louis Stutz, who was an architect for the U.S. Postal Service. He was the father-in-law of Charles T. Kurtz, the founder of Kurtz Bros., who had married his daughter, Pauline Louise Stutz in 1900, in Washington, D.C.

The Mt. Gilead Church is noted for the design of smooth dressed blocks of stone called ashlar, and for the carved decoration around the arches, windows and doors, which is paired with the coarsely dressed stone for the façade of the building. Small cherub faces are an element of the column crowns at the entry. The tower, marking the nave of the church, rises above a false gabled front which contains the central doors and a large arched window.

Inside this neighborhood church, the Romanesque motif is the defining element. Centrally balanced, the rounded arches on paired columns and a sectioned dome ceiling carry through the theme. A wooden board-and-bread ceiling with hipped profile is supported with carved brackets. The church is single-story except for the overhanging rear porch which may have been designed for the choir but is now used to seat the congregation. The pews, original to the church, curve progressively from the front to the back of the church in a sweeping dramatic arc on each side of the central aisle.

1625 13th and Corcoran Streets, Washington, D.C.

South

St. Helena's Church and Cemetery

Founded in 1712, St. Helena's is one of the oldest churches in continuous use in America. During the Revolution the British used the church as horse stables. During the Civil War it served as a two-story hospital. The raised tombstones were used as operating tables.

Beaufort, South Carolina

Field of Cotton
Route 321, South Carolina

South

Cotton-Picking Machines
These machines are a far cry from the generations of families that picked cotton by hand.

South Carolina

Cotton Farmer's Shack

This shack had once been a slave home and was also a home to tenant cotton farm families.

Outside Greensboro, Alabama

Wall Gun

It takes two men to fire this 100 mm wall gun shown at a re-enactment held at Fort King George.

South

Fort King George

This, the first English fort in Georgia, was built in 1721 to counteract French and Spanish expansion north of Florida. The fort's earthworks, buildings, and a reconstructed three-story blockhouse provide a spectacular view of the surrounding marshes and the Altamaha River.

A number of English soldiers are buried in the lonely fort's adjacent graveyard, a far distance from their homeland. Remains of three later sawmills and tabby ruins are still visible. The fort was abandoned in 1736.

Darien, Georgia

Cumberland Island National Seashore

Cumberland, one of the largest of the coastal barrier islands, once the site of treasure-smuggling pirates, is an ecological island where wild horses, boars, turkey, alligator, armadillo, deer, mink and a tremendous variety of coastal birds and other wildlife roam freely throughout the saltwater marshes, the maritime forest and along the 17 miles of secluded white sandy beaches. Live oak and palmetto forests provide shelter for much of the wildlife. Each year female loggerhead turtles come ashore to lay their eggs.

For thousands of years people have lived on the island, but never in such numbers as to permanently alter the landscape. In 1971 most of the island was given by the Carnegie family, who had large homes here, to the National Park Foundation for the establishment of the Cumberland Island National Seashore. There is a strict limit to the number of tourists permitted to visit the island at any one time. Although the Greyfield Inn provides for guests, no cars are permitted on the island.

St. Marys, Georgia

South

Adam Strain Building

This stucco tabby two-story warehouse was built in 1813-1815 as a mercantile store and ship's chandlery. It was burned by Union forces during the Civil War, but was refurbished in 1873.

Darien, Georgia

Fort Frederica National Monument

General James Edward Oglethorpe of England established Fort Frederica as a military town of 500 persons on St. Simons Island, Georgia in 1736, using it as a stronghold against Spanish encroachment. The town and Fort Frederica were the largest British military installations in the Western Hemisphere. Spain controlled St. Augustine, Florida, to the south, while England ruled over Charleston to the north. The land between was claimed by each. Wanting a buffer along her southern frontier, Britain established the colony of Georgia, the last of the thirteen, in the unoccupied territory below the Carolinas.

Although little more than a footnote in history, the importance of the Battle of Gully Hole Creek on the morning of July 7, 1742, followed later that day by the Battle of Bloody Marsh, only six miles away, succeeded in driving the Spanish out of Georgia and securing the coast north of Florida for the British. Both battles were fought with only a few hundred men and lasted only about an hour. By today's standards, the battles were small skirmishes, but at that time the control of vast tracts of land was often determined by small engagements of only a few hundred men.

These two battles become more significant when one considers that in the greater strategic sense their outcome saved the colony of Georgia for Oglethorpe and preserved an empire for England; for if Georgia had fallen, the next Spanish target would have been Charleston and the Carolinas. As it was, Spain soon became discouraged and withdrew from all of Florida. Shortly thereafter, the town of Frederica, having outlived its military purpose, ceased to exist.

Re-enactors at St. Simons Island, Georgia

South

St. Simons Island Lighthouse

The historic site of the St. Simons Lighthouse dates back to Fort St. Simons, a colonial fort, which was built under General James Oglethorpe's command to protect the southern tip of the island. The original lighthouse was built in 1804. It was blown up by Confederate forces in 1862 to prevent its use by Federal troops. The present 104-foot lighthouse and Victorian keepers dwelling were built in 1872. The light from the present-day lighthouse can be seen 18 miles out at sea.

Near the lighthouse is located an old Spanish Garden that was part of the Spanish Missions established in early 1568 along the coast of Georgia and Florida. Due to Indian uprisings, pirate raids and British plundering, these missions were moved further south in 1686.

St. Simons Island, Georgia

Tarboro Mercantile Co.
Route 17 & 252, White Oak, Georgia

South

Tarboro County Store

Started in 1910 as an outlet for the wholesale groceries of the Tarboro Mercantile Co., this store is now owned by Mark and Roxanne, who maintain the antique atmosphere of this nearly one hundred-year-old general store.

Route 252, Tarboro, Georgia

South

Sheldon Church Ruins

These ruins are all that remain of Prince William's Parish Church, once one of the most impressive in the South. Erected in 1745-55, the church was burned by British troops in 1779, rebuilt and then burned again by Union troops in 1865.

North of Beaufort, South Carolina, near Gardens Corner, 1.7 miles north of the junction of Highways 21 and 17

Route 17

As the Interstate Highway System was built, many of the formerly well traveled roads that had carried travelers for decades throughout the United States and had been so important in the building of the nation became little used except for local traffic. Often by traveling them today you encounter old abandoned businesses, especially motels, gas stations and general stores that awaken a nostalgic feeling for the past. Shown here, at the Georgia – Florida border, near the Saint Marys River, are several such scenes.

South

Fancy Honey
Route 82, near Atkinson, Georgia

Hofwyl-Broadfield Plantation

This former rice plantation is presently a 1,268-acre wildlife preserve. Beginning in 1806, slaves, many of whom were experienced in rice cultivation in Africa, developed a thriving industry in this area. The present house was built in the 1850s.

Route 17 south of Darien, Georgia

South

Home of Carl Sandburg

Carl Sandburg has been called the poet of industrial America and is considered by many to have been the chief poetical figure since the time of Walt Whitman. He wrote of the toilers, hand workers and day laborers, giving voice to the feelings and moods of America, which was on the industrial move. His subjects range from pioneer grandmothers to work-gangs, railroad men, hoboes, convicts, cowboys, mountain people including a multitude of others who lived the common, big-fisted, rough-necked life of moving America's industrial might forward. Sandburg, a Lincoln enthusiast, produced the definitive biography of our Civil War President in *The Prairie Years* and *The War Years*. His free-verse poems continue popular, and his *Remembrance Rock* novel is well worth reading.

Hendersonville, North Carolina

Great Egret

One of the show birds of the south is the sleek and dazzling great white egret. These elegant birds can often be seen wading on marsh lands, creeks, ponds and lagoons. Their beautiful plumes flare out as in a mating display.

Zoological Park at the Alligator Farm, St. Augustine, Florida

South

Ghost Crab

These ghost crabs appear on beaches mostly at night, when they scurry around on tiptoes. Their periscope-like eyes provide 360-degree vision except that they cannot see straight above them.

Grounded Tug
Little St. Simons Island, Georgia

Hazel's Cafe

The St. Simons African-American Black Heritage Coalition is preserving much of the heritage of the Georgia isle, now called the Golden Isles, near Brunswick, Georgia. For more than a century this island sheltered emancipated African-Americans. The Coalition is preserving landmarks, traditions and spaces that strengthen ancestral ties. This café was once a busy social hub.

St. Simons Island, Georgia

South

Gingerbread House
Bull and 37th Street area, Savannah, Georgia

Shrimp Boat Fleet

Photo by Marilyn Kurtz taken at the "Blessing of the Shrimp Boats" in Darien, Georgia

South

Cockspur Lighthouse

Built in the 1840s, and abandoned in the 1950s, this lighthouse is now part of the Fort Pulaski National Monument.

South Channel, Savannah River, Savannah, Georgia

Castillo de San Marcos

This Spanish fort was begun in 1672 to protect St. Augustine from British expansion. Today it stands as a symbol of Spain's early colonization of America. The city of St. Augustine, established in 1565, is the oldest permanent European settlement in the continental United States. Shown here is the San Carlos Bastion portion of the fort, which is surrounded by Matanzas Bay and a moat.

The fort was built in a hollow square with diamond shaped bastions on each corner. In 1740, after besieging the fort for 38 days, the British gave up and returned to Georgia. After the Battle of Bloody Marsh on St. Simons Island, Georgia, where the British defeated the Spanish, on July 7, 1742, Spain withdrew from all of Florida.

St. Augustine, Florida

South

City Gates

Built in 1739, this gate provided the only access through the defense line on the north side of Spanish St. Augustine. In his search for the Fountain of Youth, Juan Ponce de Leon, claiming the land for the crown of Spain, sailed around Florida, landing near St. Augustine in 1513. His voyage was only twenty-one years after that of Columbus.

Under the Big Top

All the world's a stage,
And all the men and women merely players:
They have their exits and their entrances;
And one man in his time plays many parts.
As You Like It, II, vii, 139
- William Shakespeare

Circuses have been around since before the founding of America. They crisscross the country year after year visiting towns large and small, managing to reinvent themselves when they seem on the verge of extinction. They are the embodiment of our dreams: a metaphor for ourselves. Encompassing two seemingly contradictory truths, circuses featuring performers from perhaps a dozen different countries, speaking half a dozen languages and practicing perhaps twice as many religions, while living together in one traveling community with little means of privacy or escape, are probably more exotic than you expect, and yet more wholesome than you anticipate. A circus is our imagination of Huckleberry Finn and Superman rolled into one. There is sin as

much as splendor, but in many ways, the circus is often a mirror of America.

Since the circus is part illusion, comprising mystery and fantasy, some of us can no more say goodbye to the circus than we can say goodbye to the memories of our childhood. The circus is a place in which to lose yourself and relive forgotten dreams. It is a shared illusion of escape in which both the audience and the performers are willing participants. It is part of the childhood of us all.

The thrill of the circus, with all of its color, grandeur and showmanship is a significant part of the magic shows which I used to perform, as an amateur magician, often for children's audiences, many years ago.

Virgil's Magic Performance

The magician Virgil the Great, who had performed on many continents, brought his illusion magic show, sponsored by the Lions Club, to the Lyric Theater in Clearfield on Tuesday, October 5, 1954. Virgil's show was billed as a magic circus, for that really is what all circuses and magic shows are about. I've never forgotten his show, nor my backstage visit with him that evening. Virgil, and his wife Julie, known as the Sweetheart of Magic, performed one of the greatest magic and illusion shows ever assembled. Together, they performed for 45 years, largely in small towns throughout America, but also made a grand tour of three continents in the 1950s.

"A circus is so much more splendid when performed under a tent" proclaims legendary circus owner Johnny Pugh. His Cole Bros. Circus, has been performing under tents since it began in 1884, 125 years ago.

Cole Bros. Circus, Brunswick, Georgia

Horseback Jugglers

This photo captures two juggling pins in mid-air while the jugglers ride their horses by standing bare-back.

South

Circus Clowns

These three clowns, of whom the older two are brothers, have been with Cole Bros. Circus eight and twelve years respectively. The young clown in the center is the son of the clown on the right.

The Flying Trapeze

Precise timing is essential for execution of this
mid-air triple somersault.

St. Charles Streetcar

Reminiscent of the Tennessee Williams play *A Streetcar Named Desire*.
New Orleans, Louisiana

South

Preservation Hall

This small, shabby building, with very limited seating and mostly standing room only, is the birthplace of jazz. Rhythm-and-blues, gospel, Cajun, zydeco and even rock-and-roll all owe a big debt to the Louisiana bayou.

426 St. Peter Street New Orleans, Louisiana

South

St. Louis Cathedral

The third house of worship to be built on this site, the present cathedral was completed in 1794. The garden behind the cathedral was once a notorious dueling ground.

New Orleans, Louisiana

Rob on Hay Roll
Photo by Marilyn
North Dekota

Prairie States

Prairie States

Eighmy School #9

This one-room schoolhouse was opened in 1900 and closed on January 21, 1941, with one boy in attendance. There had been five boys, but four were from the same family which moved away, prompting the closing. This school served an area of four square miles. It is one of the most picturesque schools remaining on the Iowa prairie.

Route 169, Tingley Township, Ringgold County, near the town of Clearfield, Iowa

Most of us are partial to the geographic area in which we spent the formative and impressionable years of our youth. When we've traveled to other regions of this country however, we sometimes inexplicably form a bond there too.

For whatever reason, I have a strong affinity with the prairie states, especially those in the great heartland of America: Kansas, Nebraska, and the Dakotas. The expanse and vastness of that area can sometimes be overwhelming. The grandeur of the immense sky that opens out from horizon to horizon, the history of homesteading and westward expansion carried out by the resilience, courage and selflessness of those able to brave an incredibly difficult weather, appeals to one's imagination and sense of adventure. No American writer has captured that spirit and the mystique of this particular area quite so well as Willa Cather. That is why I consider her our most eloquent pioneer writer.

Especially notable is North Dakota where there are many abandoned homes, schools and churches, a product of the population decline as family farms have given way to ever larger and more mechanized farm methods. With the advent of railroads and the frequent necessity of water for the steam engines, towns sprang up only seven or so miles apart.

Towns can be spotted from miles away as the grain elevators dominate the treeless horizon. Schools were originally placed so that students could walk to school on dirt roads or even on paths, in all types of weather. Modern transportation and population migration has changed all that.

The settlement of a large portion of the Unites States took place in this geographic region because of the passage of the Homestead Act in 1862 and the lure of a vast supply of free land which it provided. That combined with the American character traits of individualism, adventure, independence and the promise of self-sufficiency soon led to the western expansion which became known as Manifest Destiny.

Because they are passing from the scene, I have chosen to highlight a number of these buildings. It is interesting to speculate on the lives of those who lived, worked, studied and worshiped here and to consider what was their subsequent life and that of their families. Often buildings are simply abandoned, left unlocked with the only intruders being birds and other wildlife.

Calendars, newspapers and magazines, often dating to a time forty years past are sometimes left in kitchens and other rooms. One town meetinghouse had voting records of years ago on tables in the building. It is almost reminiscent of some of the Indian dwellings of the Southwest, where the inhabitants, or so it seems, suddenly left. Some of these abandoned farms are reminiscent of Andrew Wyeth's painting *"Christina's World"* and might be called *"Christina's* **Other** *World."*

Prairie States

Lincoln – Douglas Debates

Of the seven three-hour debates held in 1858 for the United States Senate seat in Illinois, between Abraham Lincoln and Stephen Douglas, the only remaining site is the Main Hall building on the campus of Knox College, where the fifth debate took place in the afternoon of October 9th. Because of bad weather, Lincoln, Douglas and the other speakers had to make their entrance onto the speaker's platform through the window shown here to the left of the door.

In the debates, Lincoln set forth the idea that no majority should be able to limit the most fundamental rights of a minority: life, liberty, and the pursuit of happiness. Douglas on the other hand saw the issue as one of self-government, by which the people of any state or territory had the right to determine whether that state or territory should remain either a free state or a slave state. Douglas defeated Lincoln for the Senate seat.

Galesburg, Illinois

Prairie States

Home of Abraham Lincoln

In May of 1844, Abraham and Mary Todd Lincoln needed more living space for their young family. They selected a Greek Revival style cottage at the corner of Eighth and Jackson Streets owned by the Reverend Charles Dresser, who had married the Lincolns in 1842. Lincoln paid $1,500 for the home the family would occupy for the next 17 years, until they moved into their next home, which would be The White House. Over the years the Lincolns made several additions, converting the cottage to a two-story house in 1855-56. After Lincoln's election they gave away or sold most of their furnishings and rented the house.

Only a simple nameplate on the door reading "A. Lincoln" tells visitors who resided therein.

Springfield, Illinois

Lincoln-Herndon Law Offices

Prairie States

Onstot Copper Shop

The six years Lincoln spent in New Salem formed a turning point in his career. From a gangling youngster who came to the village in 1831, at age 22, with no definite objectives in life, he left at age 28 to embark upon a career in law.

The Onstot Copper shop is the only original building remaining at the New Salem site. During the time he lived in New Salem, Lincoln clerked in the Onstot shop (which made buckets, tubs, barrels, and split rails), enlisted in the Black Hawk War, served as postmaster and deputy surveyor, failed in a retail business with partner William Berry and won election to the Illinois General Assembly in 1834 and 1836, after an unsuccessful attempt in 1832. In the spring of 1837, having been licensed to practice law, Lincoln moved to Springfield.

The Lincoln New Salem State Historic Site, two miles south of Petersburg and 20 miles northwest of Springfield, Illinois

Old Illinois State Capital

It was here in the old Illinois State Capitol building that Lincoln gave his House Divided speech, which was one of the most radical approaches of that time, especially concerning the nationalization of slavery. The "house divided" quotation was one familiar to virtually everyone in the Bible-reading, church-going state of Illinois. The speech did much to insure that Lincoln would be a formidable opponent to Senator Stephen H. Douglas in their upcoming senate campaign. Douglas won that election. Had Lincoln won the Senate seat, he likely would not have been the Republican Presidential nominee in 1860 and thus would never have been elected president.

Springfield, Illinois

Prairie States

Mississippi River Paddleboats
The Quad Cities of Davenport and Bettendorf, Iowa, and Moline/East Moline and Rock Island, Illinois

Prairie States

Approaching Sunset on the Mississippi

A view of what the Mississippi River must have looked like to explorers, riverboat captains, Tom Sawyer, Huckleberry Finn, Mark Twain and those others who followed.

In his book *Huckleberry Finn*, Mark Twain wrote one of the stories that have defined our national character. Samuel Clemens took the pen name of Mark Twain from his river travels. The term "mark twain" was used in navigation by the pilots on the river boats to designate that they were in "safe water." The term "twain" was a measure of the depth of the water through which they were passing. When it was "mark" twain they had marked a depth of safe water, two fathoms, or twelve feet.

Hannibal, Missouri

Tom Sawyer's Whitewashed Fence at Aunt Polly's House
Hannibal, Missouri

Prairie States

Forest Grove School

This one-room school built in 1874 served the surrounding area until the 1940s when it was closed due to school consolidation brought on by transportation and road improvements.

Forest Grove Drive, Davenport, Scott County, Iowa

Living History Farms

With exhibits spanning 300 years and five historical time periods, the Living History Farms show how the fertile prairies were transformed into the most productive farmland in the world. Included are a 1700 Ioway Indian village, an 1850 pioneer farm, the 1875 frontier town of Walnut Hill, a 1900-era working horse-powered farm which features many historic harvest machinery demonstrations as well as a modern farm center.

Urbandale, Iowa

Prairie States

1850 Pioneer Farm and Cabin

Wagon Wheels that Traversed the Prairie

Farm Wagon and Barbed Wire Fence
Nebraska

Prairie States

Malteze Cross Cabin

This cabin was used in the 1880s by Theodore Roosevelt when he spent time in the Dakotas. It was later moved to the south unit of the National Park which was named after him. Roosevelt loved the strenuous outdoor life, which he turned to after the death of his wife and mother in 1884. He claimed that he "never would have been President if it had not been for my experiences in North Dakota."

Theodore Roosevelt National Park (South Unit), North Dakota

Farm Truck

Near Vale, South Dakota

(Following Pages)

Tipi (or Tepee) Rings of Rocks

These circles of rocks, often overlooking rivers, can sometimes be found on the ridge tops and upland plains areas of eastern Montana and western North Dakota. The rocks were placed here and repeatedly reused for many generations by Indian tribes, for as long as five hundred to one thousand years, to secure their tepees to the ground while they camped, until moving on, in search of game or to a new farming area. Always the tepee door faced east.

A careful look at this picture shows the rocks placed in a twelve or fourteen-foot circle. Until horses arrived on the northern Great Plains, dogs were used to pull the tipi from campsite to campsite. Some sites had more than a dozen tipis. Note: the spelling of "tipi" is the Dakota Indian spelling of the word *tepee*.

Near Homestead (population 50), Montana

Prairie States

Buffalo Wallow

Still visible on the Great Plains are "buffalo wallows," where buffalos repeatedly perform the ritual, as this one is, of a dirt bath.

Theodore Roosevelt National Park (South Unit), North Dakota

121

North Dakota State Fair
A Proud Young Farmer

Sheep Shearing
Minot, North Dakota

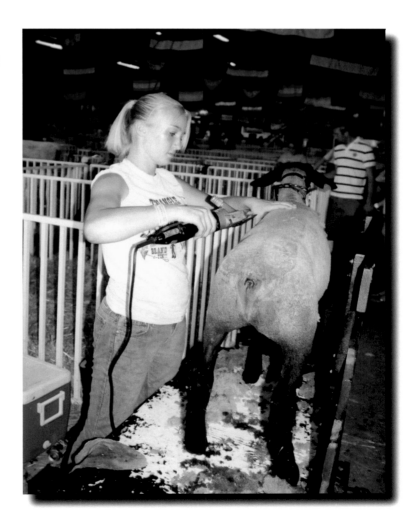

Lonely Farmstead

Church for Sale

This photograph presents an interesting perspective on the impermanence of humans and their structures, even churches.

Near Velva, North Dakota

Prairie States

Town Hall

This versatile building was built as a bank in 1916 in the town of Appam, named for Frederick W. Appam, a Great Northern Railroad surveyor. The building has served over the years as the town hall, beer hall, movie theater, farm organization meeting house, voting hall and gathering place for parties, card playing and dances. This simple structure is elevated in importance when you become aware of the multiple functions that one building plays in the life of the inhabitants of a small town. The Appam population presently is 25.

Appam, North Dakota

Wheat Thrashing Machine

An old McCormick-Deering thrashing machine from the 1930s, sometimes termed "Dinosaur of the Prairie."

Near Napoleon, North Dakota

Prairie States

Dakota Wheat Fields at Harvest Time

Rake and Abandoned Farmhouse

Until the 1960s Wayne Anderson, a young farm lad in his teens, lived on this farm. The family moved away, but his copies of *Boys' Life* magazine (published by the Boy Scouts of America) are still in this home, along with many other magazines and even newspapers from that era. The haunting quality of this scene has led some to call it "Christina's Other World without Christina," in reference to Andrew Wyeth's well-known painting, *Christina's World*.

Route 46 near Marion, North Dakota

Prairie States

Deserted Schoolhouse

These now deserted and abandoned schoolhouses were once filled with young farm children comprising many European ethnic backgrounds, cultures and languages. Their immigrant parents sought out a better living in the great farm lands of the expanding prairies.

It is difficult to imagine the happy children that may have once populated this schoolhouse. In the late 1800s and early 1900s many schools were placed only seven miles apart so that no child would have to brave the icy winters by walking too far.

Route 36, near Robinson, North Dakota

Abandoned Schoolhouse

These rusting remains of children's swings serve as a reminder of earlier, happy and lively times on the northern plains.

North Dakota

Prairie States

Wheatfield, Barn and House

Route 85, south of Belfield, North Dakota

Farmhouse
Route 53 south of Minot, at Ruso (population 6), North Dakota

Prairie States

Arena Church

Many of these churches once served as active social focal points for farming communities. The town of Arena, named for this shallow valley, was established in 1906 and enjoyed a 1920 population of 150.

Route 36, at Arena, North Dakota

One-Room Schoolhouse

In past decades, with large farm families, sometimes as few as three or four families might have enough children to keep the local school going. With today's smaller families, many local schools have closed. In earlier times the teacher might be only a few years older than the oldest pupils.

Prairie States

Abandoned Farmhouse with Hay Bales
Montana route 256 near the North Dakota border

Abandoned North Dakota Farmstead

Long-abandoned properties are often left undisturbed in the middle
of wheat fields or other crops.

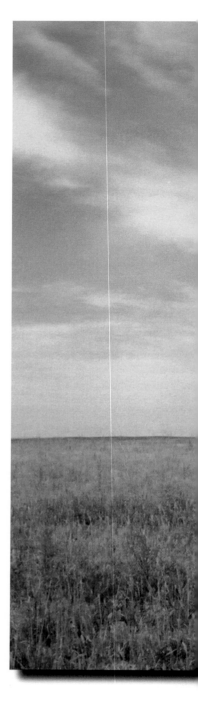

Prairie States

Abandoned House with Collapsed Porch
Near Appam, North Dakota

Red Grain Elevator
Raymond (population 12), Montana

Prairie States

Leaning Twin Grain Elevators

As farm children are educated and move on for greater opportunity to large towns and cities, the small, once flourishing farming communities are decimated by the loss of population.

Near Arena, North Dakota

Twin Grain Elevators

Route 21 near Carson, North Dakota

139

Trucks in Montana Field

Prairie States

Wheatfield at Crossroads Schoolhouse

On Route 18, along what is known as the "Hi-Line" or northern border with Canada, this North Dakota school is surrounded by swaying grass and golden wheat.

Church

Antelope (population 65), Montana

Schoolhouse

It is surprising how many of the abandoned schools, churches and homes have managed to survive the rigorous winter weather. Often the forces of nature have caused more deterioration than vandalism.

Gascoyne (population 23), North Dakota

Prairie States

Fort Union Trading Post

This 1828 site was the earliest trading post on the upper Missouri River. Located at the junction with the Yellowstone River, it was in the heart of the Indian and fur-trading country.

Near Williston, North Dakota, at the Montana border

Great Plains Dust Bowl

In the midst of the great Depression of the 1930s, the American Plains area was experiencing an extreme drought with heavy windstorms. During the expansion of farming in the 1920s, millions upon millions of acres were turned from grasslands that had held the precious top soil in place, into productive farm land. Violent winds came in the 1930s blowing much of the topsoil away, leaving little fertile ground for growing crops. So violent was the wind, and so slight was the rain, and so terrible the record-breaking heat over that decade, that the dust storms carried topsoil as far east as Washington and New York City, with even the entire sun being blotted out at noonday. Only at the end of that decade was erosion control practiced at all.

The Great Dust Bowl, as it was called, extended throughout the mid-west with the epicenter from Nebraska through the Texas Panhandle and included the Dakotas as well as eastern New Mexico. The resulting migration, although most farmers remained where they were, became known as Okies, as they moved westward in search of farming jobs.

This colorful part of our history led to the great documentary photography of Walker Evans and Dorothea Lange. Today it is almost unbelievable that entire farm buildings were covered over with dust while many people actually had to shovel the dust and dirt out of their homes while yet others became trapped in their houses as dust piled up against doors and windows, not once but many times during these years.

On the following pages are pictures of lonely homes and schools which were abandoned during the Dust Bowl era or shortly thereafter.

Two of the best factual books on the era of the dust bowl are *The Worst Hard Time* by Timothy Egan, published by Mariner, a division of Houghton Mifflin Company, and the compilation of the diary of Don Hartwell by Marsha Davis, to be published under the title of *One Man's Voice: The Don Hartwell Diary*.

Prairie States

Scenes from Edmond, Kansas, once a flourishing town
which now has a population of 47

Prairie States

In the United States there is more space where nobody is than where anybody is. That is what makes America what it is.

- Gertrude Stein

Other scenes from the dust bowl era on the Great Plains

Prairie States

151

Teton Mountains
Views along Antelope Flats Road adjacent to Grand Teton National Park.
Wyoming

Prairie States

Wyoming Meadow

Anasazi is the name given to the prehistoric Indians who inhabited the Four Corners area of the Southwest-southeastern Utah, northeastern Arizona, southwestern Colorado, and northwestern New Mexico for a 2,000-year period beginning about 700 B.C.

The name Anasazi translates from a Navajo term which has the generally accepted meaning of "ancient peoples." The kiva was a religious ceremonial structure, usually round and partly underground. A pueblo is a communal dwelling consisting of contiguous flat-roofed stone or adobe houses in groups, often several stories high. Today's Navajo, Hopi, Ute and Zuni tribes are descendants of the Anasazi. With no written records for historians to consult, interpretations of their culture vary dramatically.

Marilyn at Chaco Canyon Ruins, New Mexico

Southwest

Navajo National Monument

The magnificent cliff dwellings of Betatakin and Keet Seel (sometimes spelled Kiet Siel), both located in the Navajo National Monument, in the remote Tesgi Canyon sector of the Navajo reservation, are two of the largest and best preserved cliff houses in the Southwest. Both require some planning and commitment of time and energy on the part of those who would explore them fully.

The photographs on this and the following twelve pages were taken in late March 1956 when I was a college student. Although taken over 50 years ago, with the camera and film of that era, they are some of the best pictures I have ever produced. Several turned out better than the ones made when I returned years later. The reason was the time of year, the position of the sun and the time of day. Sometimes that makes all the difference!

My 1956 trip through this section of Arizona and Utah, comprising the Four Corners area of the Southwest, to Sunset Crater, Wupatki, Navajo National Monument and the Betatakin Ruin, on through Monument Valley and north as far as Bluff, Utah, was possible, in 1956, only on unpaved dirt, sand and gravel roads, often resembling a wash board, making the 250-mile trip an incredible adventure by today's standards.

Southwest

Road to Monument Valley

Showing Agathl Peak

Monument Valley, part of the Colorado Plateau, is not a valley in the conventional sense, but rather a wide, flat and desolate landscape, interrupted by the crumbling sandstone formations, some rising hundreds of feet into the air. These are the last remnants of what once covered the region.

1954 Ford at Arizona-Utah Border

View of Tesgi Canyon

For a short time during the thirteenth century, the Anasazi retreated to cliff dwellings in the sandstone canyons. Rock shelters often were excellent places in which to live. By 1250, the population of the area began to concentrate in Tsegi Canyon and there build cliff dwellings in the alcoves. Betatakin and nearby Kiet Siel were built at this time. However, by the 1280s, and most certainly by 1300, within a few generations of time, these spectacular sites had been abandoned.

Southwest

Betatakin Cliff Dwelling Overlook

This multi-story pueblo ruin of more than 130 rooms exhibits stone masonry and adobe brick and jacal construction. The site consists of living and storage rooms, ceremonial religious rooms (kivas), and courtyards.

Betatakin Ruin at Navajo National Monument

Of all the Anazini ruins in the Southwest, the Betatakin Ruin is probably the most dramatic and inspirational. There may be better ruins, larger ruins, or more intact ruins, but the impressive site of Betatakin, coupled with its relative inaccessibility and solitude, makes it one of the most picturesque ruins in the Southwest. It's a rugged and strenuous five-mile hike, deep into the canyon to visit the ruin, but well worth the trip. Built in the 1260s and 1270s Betatakin was occupied for only a few generations. The park service conducts limited daily tours from May through September. *(Following Pages)*

Betatakin Corn Grinding Bins

Southwest

Detail of Betatakin Ruin

Indian Hogan

On that March 1956 day, since I was the only visitor to the Betatakin ruin, the ranger gave me a private late afternoon tour. He further invited me to unroll my sleeping bag and spend the night, which I did in the Indian hogan, shown above.

Southwest

Anasazi Sunrise Above Betatakin

This sunrise photo was taken in the earliest of a
March morning, just after I had stepped out of my
overnight stay in the Indian hogan.

Wupatki National Monument

In this area the sky is an overwhelming presence, signaling the length of days, phases of the moon and the changing of the seasons. Between 1130 and 1192, up to 3,000 people lived in the Wupatki area.

60 miles east of the Grand Canyon and 15 miles north of Sunset Crater, Arizona

Southwest

Monument Valley Totem Pole

View of Monument Valley Formations with Totem Pole on the Left

Double Arches
Arches National Park, Utah

Southwest

Balanced Rock

Arches National Park, Utah

Sunset Crater Volcano

Rising 1,000 feet above the desert floor, 60 miles east of the Grand Canyon, is Sunset Crater. It was created by a series of volcanic eruptions over a 130-year span, starting about 1064. It is rare in the sense that it is one of the longest-lived cinder cone volcanoes known. Most of the surrounding lava and cinders have been preserved due to the lack of rainfall in the Southwest. Prior to 1973 (now forbidden) anyone could climb the volcano, which I did in 1956. Looking west from the top, one can perceive the magnificent volcanic mountains of the San Francisco Peaks, which were created millions of years before Sunset Crater.

Arizona

Southwest

Indian Dancers
Santa Fe, New Mexico

View of Canyonlands National Park, Utah
(Following Pages)

San Miguel Mission

Built in 1610, this is the oldest church structure in the
United States.

Santa Fe, New Mexico

Southwest

Santa Rosa de Lima Church Ruin
Route 84, south of Abiquiu, New Mexico

Shiprock in an Approaching Storm
Through Shiprock rises more than 1,700 feet above the desert, it is dwarfed by the looming storm clouds. This is a sacred place to the Navajo Indians.

Shiprock, New Mexico

Church Rock
Route 456, northeast corner, New Mexico

Southwest

Painted Desert

This part of the desert badlands exhibits brightly colored mineral hues.

East of Holbrook, Arizona

Aztec Ruins

One of the largest and best preserved Anasazi pueblo ruins in the Southwest, this was built about A.D. 1100 and with nearly 500 rooms. The Aztec name was a misnomer applied by early settlers who related the ruins to the Aztecs. The Great Kiva, or religious center, is the only one of its size restored in North America. This ruin was probably an outlander to Chaco Canyon, the center for Anasazi culture, sixty miles to the south.

Aztec, New Mexico

Southwest

Laguna Mission
Interstate 40, exit at Laguna, New Mexico

Southwest

Ruins of the Mission San Geronimo de Taos

Established about 1598, this mission was burned by the Pueblos in their 1680 rebellion with only the bell tower, shown here, remaining. The Mission was later restored and then destroyed again by U. S. troops during the revolt of 1847.

Taos, New Mexico

San Rafall Church
La Cueva, New Mexico

Southwest

Santa Rosa de Lima Chapel and Cemetery

An early 1800s chapel

Santa Rosa, New Mexico

Coronado River Crossing

A few of the original crossing stones still remain at this place in the Gallinas River where the explorer Vasquez de Coronado made his crossing in 1541 while on the Spanish exploration to discover the "Seven Cities of Gold." Finding little gold, he nevertheless followed his dream as far east as the vast and desolate windswept plains of central Kansas.

Ten miles south of Santa Rosa at Puerto de Luna, New Mexico

Southwest

La Iclesia de San Acacio
New Mexico

Fencepost, Boot and Flowers

Southwest

Taos Barn

Sheep in Monument Valley

Western Corral

This corral is behind the Hubble Trading Post National Historic Site.

The still active trading post has been the meeting ground of two cultures – that of the Navajo and that of the settlers who came to the area, in what is now northeastern Arizona, in the late 1800s.

Route 264, west of Window Rock, at Ganado, Arizona

Grand Canyon
Arizona

Southwest

Helicopter View of the Colorado River
Grand Canyon, Arizona

191

Wigwam Trading Post
Route 160, Mancos, Colorado

Southwest

Chimney Rock Kiva

The Chimney Rock Archaeological Area provides a commanding view of the western foothills of the southern Rockies. Archaeological surveys in this area have turned up hundreds of sites of prehistoric Indians, spanning a long period of time including that of the pre-Anasazi Basketmaker people dating as far back as A.D. 450.

Route 160, 35 miles east of Durango, Colorado

Chimney Rock Archaeological Site

This dramatic rock formation which was a familiar landmark to Indians, pioneers and fur trappers gives the Chimney Rock site its name.

Bent's Old Fort

Located on the banks of the Arkansas River, which at the time marked the boundary between Mexico and the United States, this important fur-trading post, American Indian rendezvous, and advance base in the war with Mexico, was a way station on the Mountain Route of the Santa Fe Trail. Built in 1833, it is located two thirds of the way west, between Independence, Missouri, and Santa Fe, New Mexico. It resembles a walled town, complete with frontier necessities. The fort was abandoned in 1849.

Route 194, northeast of La Junta, Colorado

Southwest

El Morro National Monument

The El Morro Mesa provides beautiful southwest scenery and is interesting for its historical and cultural interchange. At the top of the mesa is the Atsinna Pueblo ruin with five hundred rooms arranged around an interior courtyard. The mesa itself was a geographical landmark for explorers, of whom many carved their names at the base of the rock, where water runoff provided an especially welcome respite. One of the early names carved at Inscription Rock is that of Juan de Onate, April 16, 1605.

Route 53, 42 miles southeast of Grants, New Mexico

Pine Tree Growing from Canyon Floor

From deep in a canyon this pine tree has been growing toward the sunlight, straight up, for many years.

Bryce National Park, Utah

Southwest

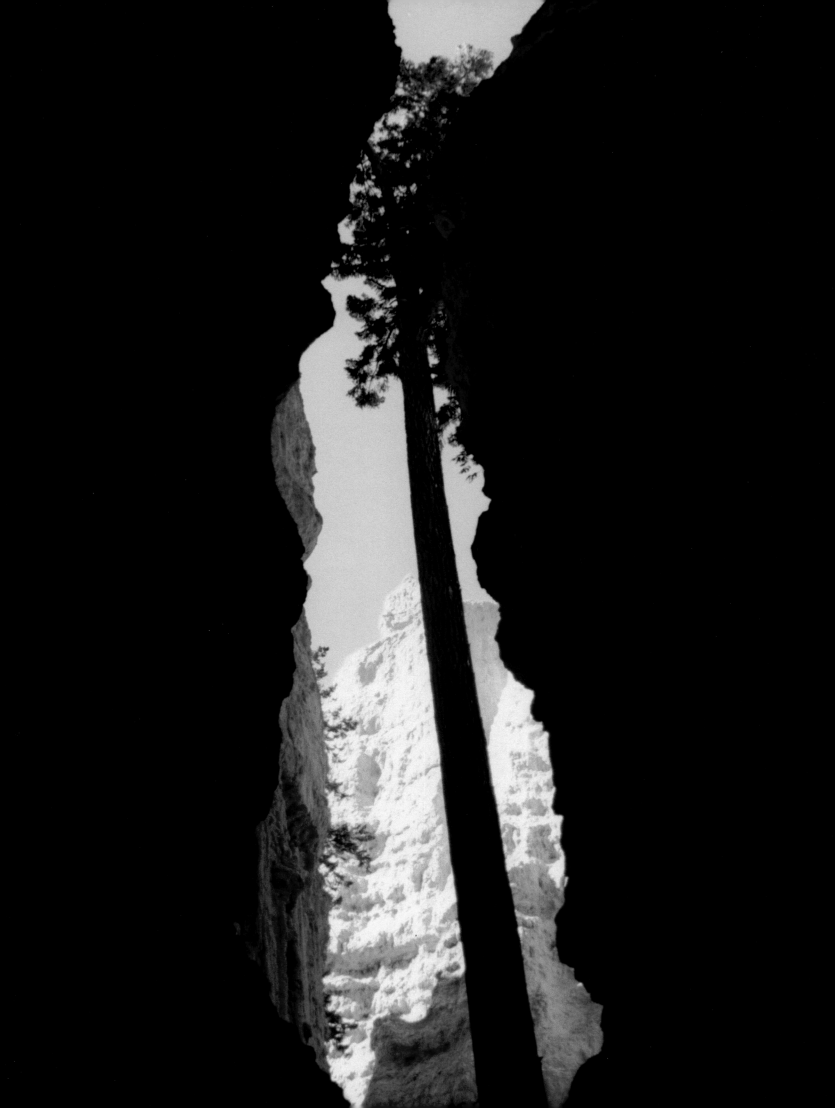

Casamero Pueblo Ruins

These pueblo ruins, dating from A.D. 1000 to 1125, are located fifty miles north of Chaco and are regarded as one of more than a hundred Chacoan outliers radiating out in all directions from that important Anasazi cultural and religious center. Although archaeologists are not sure of the relationship or how exactly to define it, they recognize a close connection between the monumental sites in Chaco Canyon and Casamero. The similarities in site layout, architectural details, the presence of a great kiva and two Chacoan roads all point to the connection between this ruin and other Chacoan outliers.

Interstate 40, Prewitt exit, 19 miles west of Grants, New Mexico

Southwest

Quarai Salinas Pueblo Missions

These pueblos and missions were built by Indians who were forced by the Spanish Franciscan priests, supported by soldiers, to build these missions in the early 1600s. And they were abandoned in the 1670s.

Three locations in central New Mexico

One of the largest, most dramatic and important of all Anasazi ruins is to be found in Chico Canyon. This was the cultural, religious and economic power center of the Anasazi world. Consisting of many clusters of separate ruins, this is one of the major areas for archaeological research in the southwest. Beginning as early as 700 B.C., Chaco's building became most active about 1030 and continued at a frenzied pace until reaching its peak as a religious center, about 1140.

Southwest

Scenes from Chaco Canyon

Until recently Chaco could be reached only by traversing many miles of rough and rutted roads. Recently a paved road has changed all that with the result that hordes of tourists have suddenly poured into the area.

It has become increasingly difficult to stabilize these, and similar ruins, when tourists and bus loads of school children lug backpacks and even coolers inside the ruins. As one teacher painfully explained to a park ranger, her students might require food and drink during his talk! Even crumbs of food, inadvertently left behind, attract rodents, which over time, act to destabilize the ruins.

Chaco Canyon National Historic Park, New Mexico

Tent Rocks

This National Monument of complex geologic scenery has seen human occupation spanning 4,000 years. The cone-shaped tent rock formations are the product of volcanic eruptions that occurred six to seven million years ago. Wind and water cut into these deposits creating canyons and arroyos. Several Indian pueblos were established nearby. In 1540, the Spanish explorer Francisco Vasquez de Coronado and his troops mentioned the unusual formations in their diaries.

South of Santa Fe, off Interstate 26, then route 22 west (or north) beyond Cochiti Pueblo, New Mexico

Southwest

Church at Golden

This little mission church was built in the early 1830s. The town has a lonely aspect, nearly lost as it is in the overwhelming vastness of the New Mexico landscape. Once boasting a population of 3,000, the community now accommodates only 14 families.

Route 14, known as the Turquoise Trail Road, Golden, New Mexico

Isleta Mission

I-25 south of Albuquerque at Isleta, New Mexico

Pecos National Historic Park

This park preserves the ruins of a large ancient pueblo as well as two massive adobe mission churches shown here, which the Franciscans forced the Indians to build in the 1600s and 1700s. From these ruins, the valley descends gradually eastward, to open on the southern Great Plains.

Off I-25, 25 miles east of Santa Fe, at Pecos, New Mexico

Southwest

Slot Canyons

These are very narrow canyons which have been washed out below the surface of the earth. Only a very limited amount of light ever enters, but that light illuminates the colorful sandstone walls. Because the canyons are so very narrow, rain storms, sometimes from many miles away, can cause flash floods which, without warning will fill the slot canyon, sweeping away everything in their path.

Near Page, Arizona

Southwest

Martinez Hacienda

This is thought to be the only restored hacienda open to the public. It was built in 1804 by Padre Antonio Severino Martinez. The fortress-like house includes 21 rooms built around two large patios.

Taos, New Mexico

Landscape Arch in Arches National Park
Utah

Southwest

Four Faces Petroglyphs

209

Southwest

Great Sand Dunes National Monument

This park of 39 square-miles in its, stark yet ever-changing sandscape provides an eerie foreground for the nearby 13,000-foot Sangre de Cristo mountain range. The park is home to America's tallest sand dunes, some towering up to 750 feet into the sky!

Thirty-eight miles northeast of Alamosa, Colorado, on Route 150

Far West

San Luis Rey Mission

Strange as it seems today, Spain established twenty-one missions along the southern California coast all in response to the territorial encroachment of Russia. Spain soon realized that large tracts of land could be inexpensively claimed by sending a few dedicated padres with a handful of soldiers and supplies to establish a mission. San Luis Rey was founded in 1798.

Oceanside, California

Far West

San Juan Capistrano Mission

The Capistrano Mission features elaborate and beautiful gardens. It was founded by the Spanish on November 1, 1776, and is thus one of the earlier California missions.

San Juan Capistrano, California

Far West

Joshua Tree National Park

This southern California National Park comprises the Mojave Desert at a higher elevation than the adjacent Colorado Desert. Like islands in a sultry sea, these two desert ecosystems show sharp contrasts.

Far West

University of Redlands

This view of the Campus Quad, shows the Memorial Chapel, of Georgian design, in the background. The focal point of the campus, this chapel serves as a meeting place for university and community functions.

Redlands, California

Oh, East is East, and West is West, and never the
Twain shall meet,
Till Earth and Sky stand presently at God's great
Judgment Seat;
But there is neither East nor West, nor border, nor
breed, nor birth,
When two strong men stand face to face, though
They come from the ends of the earth!

The Ballad of East and West
- Rudyard Kipling

HISTORIC ENGLAND

America draws its heritage from many cultures, but none can make so strong a claim upon the development, nor has any had so lasting an influence upon these shores as that of Great Britain (which term I use to include Scotland and Wales). American heritage owes more to England than to any other people or culture in the world. Language and literature, government and law, even religious and similar thought patterns prevail throughout the values and culture of both countries.

In the pages that follow, I hope to provide a perspective of Historic England that has over many centuries influenced this side of the Atlantic. Though the countries are separated by three thousand miles of ocean, and reached only by a rigorous journey, that took the Pilgrims four months, these photographs are mostly the result of a four-weeks driving trip throughout England which Marilyn and I made in the summer of 2002, the 50th year of the reign of Queen Elizabeth II.

Canterbury

The very name Canterbury conjures up images of 14th century medieval England and the English poet, Geoffrey Chaucer, with his colorful characters in the *Canterbury Tales*, as they journey from London towards the shrine of St. Thomas Becket at Canterbury Cathedral. To reread the *Canterbury Tales* is a refreshing surprise and makes one realize how little human nature has changed since Chaucer lived in the late 1300s. The town of Canterbury provides an impression of what once was medieval England.

Across The Seas

Chartwell

It was here in Kent, at the estate called Chartwell, which he purchased in 1922, that Winston Churchill spent as much time as possible, with the exception of the Second World War years, until his death in 1965. Here he lived with his beloved wife Clementine, while he wrote, painted, gardened and built brick walls. His World War II leadership left the most lasting legacy of any political leader who lived during the twentieth century.

As England's Prime Minister during the bleak WW II years, with the German army only 22 miles across the English Channel and with German air superiority pounding London, Churchill told the English people that his leadership could offer them only "blood, toil, tears and sweat." He made the prophecy that if the British Empire lasted a thousand years, men would say that the WWII years would be "their finest hour."

Historic England

English Gardens

English gardens are always a joy to behold. Even the smallest plot of ground with anything in bloom passes for a garden. Some of the best gardens are found around old castles, like those shown here at both Sissinghurst and Scotney Castle Gardens in southern England near Canterbury.

Battle of Hastings

In the year 1066, one of the most influential military campaigns in the history of the English speaking world took place. Called The Battle of Hastings, it is the dramatic story of the English King Harold Godwinson (1022-1066) the Earl of Wessex and William "the Conqueror" (1027-1087) Duke of Normandy, who engaged in their bitter, bloody quest for the crown and destiny of England. The victory of William forever changed the face of England. It was with Norman rule under William that England's castles were built. Harold was the last Anglo-Saxon king to rule. The Bayeux Tapestries depict the battle in wonderful detail. Today, more than nine centuries later, another of William's descendants reigns as England's monarch.

The battle took place on October 14, 1066, on the bloody slope of Senlac Ridge, near Hastings. King Harold, well prepared to repulse the invasion across the English Channel by William, would probably have been successful had it not been for a Viking invasion, only days before, in northern England at Samford Bridge near York. Harold quickly and successfully moved his troops north, repulsing that invasion.

Taking less than a week, Harold hastily returned south to face William, who for his invasion chose that moment, after waiting on the coast of France for most of the summer and fall, for favorable winds to carry his ships safely across the channel, took that opportunity to invade England. Had he not done so, winter weather would have soon set in and the invasion might never have taken place.

Historic England

Holy Trinity Church, Bosham

The Holy Trinity Church in Bosham, England, is one of the best examples of Saxon, Norman and Early English (dating to the 12th century) architecture. This was a religious site going back for 1600 years to Roman times. Roman bricks, artifacts and pottery have been unearthed here. A child's coffin, traditionally believed to be that of the infant daughter of King Canute (1016-1035), is buried in the church. While it is known that King Harold worshiped in this church, the notion that he was buried here after the Battle of Hastings in 1066 remains a myth.

Rastormel Castle

This circular romantic castle sits high on a ridge, surrounded by a moat, overlooking the Cornwall landscape.

Reglan Castle

Historic England

Avebury Stone Circle

Stone circles appear in many parts of England. Most are older than the pyramids, having been built during the Bronze Age between 2600 and 2100 B.C. Many circles form a remarkably accurate celestial calendar. While Stonehenge, 20 miles away, is the best known, others, while not as dramatic, afford much greater access. This stone circle at Avebury, which is sixteen times the size of Stonehenge, is far less touristy, and, for many, more interesting, since one can walk among the 100 stones, ditches, mounds, and curious patterns from the past, as well as visit the village of Avebury, which grew up in the middle of this fascinating 1,400-foot-wide neolithic stone circle.

Castlerigg Stone Circle

These 38 stones, 90 feet across and at least 3,000 years old, are mysteriously laid out on a line between the two tallest peaks on the horizon. Whatever the purpose of stone circles, and much is open to conjecture, they probably had a multiplicity of uses. What was one man's marketplace may have been another man's temple. Sheep grazed within many of the stone circles visited.

Near Keswick in the Lake District

Historic England

City of Bath and Bath Cathedral

Historic England

Stonehenge

Two views of the mammoth stones used to construct the best
known stone circle. Some appreciation of the stone size can be
gained by a close look at the people shown in the background.

Dove Cottage

William Wordsworth, the poet whose appreciation of nature and back-to-basics lifestyle put the Lake District on the map, spent his most productive years, 1799-1808, in this well preserved old cottage on the edge of Grasmere. The Lake District was also home to Coleridge and later Beatrix Potter.

Panoramic of the Lake District

Historic England

Thomas Hardy Cottage

This is the thatched roof home of Thomas Hardy, the well-known English writer who designed it and lived here from 1885 until his death in 1928. His novels, considered some of the finest in the English language, include *Tess of the D'Urbervilles, Far from the Madding Crowd* and *The Return of the Native.*

Tintern Abbey

Founded in 1131 on a site chosen by Norman monks for its tranquility, Tintern
Abbey functioned as an austere Cistercian abbey until its dissolution by Henry VIII
in 1536. Its ruins were the inspiration for the beautiful ode by William Wordsworth.

Historic England

View of the Moors

The moors are a vast area of open rolling infertile land of very spongy and low growing grasses into which one can sink well up to the ankles. It is best walked across on well-worn paths.

Hutton-le-Hole

As in many English rural areas, sheep grazed throughout this village in the Moors. The Ryedale Folk Museum, which illustrates farm life in the Moors, is located here.

Historic England

Rievaulx Abbey

A highlight of the North York Moors, this Abbey is beautifully situated in the valley of the River Rye. Founded in 1132, it prospered for 400 years until it was suppressed in 1538 during the reign of Henry VIII, who saw himself as supreme ruler answerable only unto God. Its grandeur as one of the finest and largest monastic churches in the north of England can be read in the exquisite masonry of its ruined buildings.

Walls of Saint Mary's Abbey in York

Byland Abbey

This abbey is unique in that much
of the floor tile work is still intact.

Scottish Cows

In Scotland, the word *cow* is pronounced *coo*. Even with their horns, these animals seem very lovable.

Historic England

Hadrian's Wall

About A.D. 122, during the reign of Emperor Hadrian, the Romans, having invaded England in A.D. 43, decided to build this wall to define the northern edge of the Roman empire and to protect Roman Britain from invading Scottish tribes to the north. The wall stretches 74 miles across the narrowest part of northern England. It was built and defended by 20,000 troops. Some ruins of the Roman military installations, including the army latrine, shown at left, are clearly in evidence.

Roman Fortress Ruins in York Park

York and the Old City Stone Gate

Next to London, York is the most enjoyable and historic city in all of England. Everything is within easy walking distance in this city dating to Roman times. It was here that Constantine the Great (274-337), who later founded Constantinople, was made Roman Emperor in AD 306. His recognition of the civil liberties of his Christian subjects, as well as his own conversion to the Faith, established the religion of Western Christendom.

In AD 800 the Vikings invaded this part of England. The stone gate shown here was the main gate of the Roman fortress in York.

Historic England

York Minster

York Minster (meaning a center of Christian teaching or ministering) is the largest medieval structure in England. The present cathedral, begun in 1220 and finished in 1472, is the fourth church built on the site. Roman foundations are visible under the present church.

Historic England

Historic England

Market Hall

Nestled in the Cotswolds, the town of Chipping Campden is as near to a picture-perfect village as you are likely to find. It is a working market town, home to wealthy wool merchants and features incredibly beautiful thatched roofs. The Market Hall, built in 1627, is still used and is located in the center of town.

Bury St. Edmunds Abbey and the Magna Carta

In medieval times the Abbey of Bury St. Edmunds drew pilgrims from across Europe. The Abbey was built between 1120 and 1148. On November 20, 1214, Cardinal Langton and a group of twenty-five English Barons met here. They swore, at the abbey altar, that they would obtain from King John the ratification of a charter to define their rights. This later became known as the Magna Carta, which distinguished it from the equally important (at that time), but much shorter Forest Charter.

Historic England

Runnymede

This meadow on the banks of the River Thames near Windsor Castle is where, on June 15, 1215, twenty-five barons assembled, nearly a year after their meeting at Bury St. Edmunds Abbey. Here they prevailed upon King John to sign the Great Charter, better known by its Latin name, the Magna Carta. While the exact spot in the meadow where the sealing took place is unknown, we do know that it was not on the island in the Thames, as some erroneously believe.

The Magna Carta checked the despotic power of King John and gave rights to the Barons, who were disenchanted with his wars and heavy taxes to support those wars. It set forth the privileges of the aristocracy and the Church, but did not give those same rights to the majority of common Englishmen. While this did not establish democracy as we know it, it provided the basis for English Law and the constitutional government which would follow over the ensuing centuries.

Church of Saint Mary the Virgin St. Remigius Church

This church was built in 1160. The tower is the largest Saxon round tower in Britain to be composed of flint, a mineral found in abundance in this area. In the east window are medallions of Medieval stained glass in the form of a cross. It is interesting to note that the church registers are complete from 1538.

The chancel contains memorials to the Betts family who lived at Wortham Manor for 425 years. This family took up residence in the nineteenth year of Edward IV's reign (1480), with the last member living until 1905. Documents dating from 1272 were found in a small secret room of the manor and provide historical data of the area as well as the church.

It is believed that the Betts family who came to America in 1639 came from this village of Wortham and were members of this church. Memorials to several of the Bettses are preserved on the walls, windows and floor of the church. The inside photos show both ends of the church.

Historic England

Looking from
the Nave of the Church
toward the Altar

Looking from the Nave
toward the rear of
the Church

Full many a gem of purest ray serene
The dark unfathomed caves of ocean bear;
Full many a flower is born to blush unseen,
And waste its sweetness on the desert air.

Some village Hampton that with dauntless breast
The little tyrant of his fields withstood;
Some mute inglorious Milton here may rest,
Some Cromwell guiltless of his country's blood.

Elegy Written in a Country Churchyard
- Thomas Gray

Historic England

Stoke Poges

In the cemetery of this country church, Thomas Gray wrote what has been described as the most widely read and best loved poem in the English language, the *Elegy Written in a Country Churchyard*.

The poem owes its tremendous appeal to three main features: (1) Its form is simple. (2) The music of its verse is irresistibly wistful and melancholy, but not morose. (3) More than anything else it emphasizes the importance of each individual no matter how simple or insignificant that person may be. Lincoln quoted it, Daniel Webster, on his deathbed asked his son to read it to him, Gouverneur Morris, the author of the U. S. Constitution, quoted it the day he died, it inspired Willa Cather to write the three memorable short stories entitled *Obscure Destinies*, and Samuel Johnson said that "It abounds with images which find a mirror in every mind and sentiments to which every bosom returns an echo." In 1771 Thomas Gray was buried in the churchyard.

Galapogos Islands

Galapagos Islands, Ecuador

Lying 600 miles off the Pacific coast of Ecuador, the Galapagos Islands are the jewel of the extensive Ecuadorian national park system. Explored by Charles Darwin in 1835, the islands became famous with his theory of evolution, defined in his book *The Origin of Species*. These nineteen beautiful islands are home to many unique animals, most of which have no natural predators. As a result they are unbelievably tame. Most are not found anywhere else in the world. Visitors are free to interact and even swim and snorkel with the wildlife, but are not permitted to touch any animal, tame as they may be.

Blue-footed and red-footed boobies, as well as sea lions, fur seals, dolphins, whales, rays, sea turtles, iguanas, frigate birds and Sally Lightfoot crabs abound. Here are the giant tortoises and land iguanas.

Sally Lightfoot Crab

Galapogos Islands

Frigate Bird

This male frigate bird is in full mating display.

Baby Albatross

Giant Tortoise

Sea Lion

Galapogos Islands

Blue-Footed Boobies

In an elaborate mating dance, the male proudly displays his wonderful blue feet to his female, who in turn admires them.

South of France

Avignon City Wall

Some of the best preserved Roman ruins in the world are in the Provence area of southern France, especially in and around the city of Avignon in which the old town is still contained in a defensive wall built in the 14th century. Avignon, on the Rhone River, was the center of the Catholic world and home to the Popes from 1309 to 1376. The Palais des Popes looms high above the town wall.

Truncated Bridge Span

This overlooks the bridge span known as the Pont d'Avignon, also called the Pont St-Benezet. Built from 1177 to 1185, it ends in mid-stream on the Rhone River, having been partly destroyed by flood waters.

South of France

Palais des Popes

Dominating the city of Avignon, this splendid castle was residence to several Popes from 1309 to 1376.

Pont du Gard

This Roman aqueduct is perhaps the crown jewel of the Roman ruins in France. It carried water even before the birth of Christ. Towering 150 feet above the Gardon River gorge, the aqueduct, part of a 31-mile system, is noted for the beauty of its graceful architecture and is impressive for the precision of its engineering.

South of France

Les Arenes

This Roman amphitheater, located in Arles, which was built in the 1st century, seats 25,000 and still hosts summer bullfights. It is one of the most extensive Roman ruins in France, and is in a much better state of preservation than the Coliseum in Rome.

Around the World in Thirty Days

Highlights from a trip to five continents, and ten countries reflecting ten distinct cultures and requiring 36,000 miles of travel in 30 days, including twice across the equator, are shown in the following pages.

Around The World

Around the world

Easter Island, Chile

More than 2,300 miles off the coast of Chile, remote Easter Island's sophisticated society developed from about A.D. 400 until the mid 1600s, probably by Polynesians. It then disappeared, leaving an archaeological legacy of ancient stone villages, open-air sanctuaries and 600 giant statues called moai, scattered around the island.

These tall, brooding figures, some weighing up to 250 tons and 30 to 50 feet in height, were carved from dense volcanic tuff, transported to the coast and raised onto great stone altars called ahu. In many places, the seashore is lined with these stone idols, all positioned with their backs turned to the sea.

Nearly 400 unfinished figures were mysteriously abandoned. Easter Island stands outside the trade routes of the world, quiet and remote, with its story still unexplained.

267

Papua, New Guinea

Located northeast of Australia, New Guinea is an island of hundreds of distinct tribal cultures that follow the ancient traditions of their Stone Age ancestors. Many of the tribes had never seen a non-islander until ten years ago. In the deepest interior parts, it is still believed that some tribes have never had any outside contact and may have no knowledge of the world beyond their own tribal domain.

The impenetrable jungle and jagged mountain ranges have kept New Guinea's many tribes isolated from each other and from the rest of the world. As a result, there are over 700 different and distinct languages and tribal cultures in a population of just over three million in a country only slightly larger than California.

Around the world

The Huli Wigmen

The most convenient way to get around the island is by aircraft. That and a three-hour truck ride over the most primitive of roads took us to the Huli tribe, whose colorful self-decoration is the most striking in New Guinea. The Huli Wigmen sport huge wigs of their own hair.

It is such a tribal honor to be chosen to become a Wigman that they cannot marry and must sleep in a partially upright position to protect their wigs. When we arrived, hundreds of natives stood outside the airstrip to witness the landing of our small single-engine plane. Our truck ride took us far into the interior, where cameras and photographs are nearly unheard of. Toilets are a hole in the ground, with no place to sit.

As a gesture to Western ways, women were recently permitted to take part in the sing-sing dances once performed only by men. This unfortunately highlights how we are willing agents to the destruction of their culture, all done in the name of progress and our own tendency to enforce political correctness on other cultures. It is a shame that we permit our Western prejudices to corrupt their culture in this way.

Around the world

Angkor Wat, Cambodia

Built to the Hindu God Vishnu
between 900 A.D. and 1,300 A.D.
the great temple of Angkor Thom
and its companion, Angkor Wat
(shown here in a photo by
Marilyn Kurtz). The ancient capital
of the Khmer Empire and the world's
largest religious complex are one
of the world's great architectural
achievements.

The massive temple complex of
soaring towers, elaborately carved
murals, colonnades and courtyards
ushered in the classic age of Khmer
art and architecture.

These temples are believed to have
been inhabited by one million
people, more than the number in
any European city of that time.
They were protected from pillage
and encroaching vegetation by
Buddhist monks who lived there
after the Khmers moved their capital
to Phnom Penh in the mid-15th
century. For centuries Angkor was
virtually unknown to the outside
world.

Around the world

Taj Mahal

Agra is the 16th-century capital of India's Mogul Empire. Here Emperor Shah Jahan built an everlasting tribute to his deceased wife. The shimmering white-marble of the Taj Mahal, built from 1632 to 1643, is one of the world's great architectural masterpieces. This monument to eternal love sits atop a great marble terrace in an expansive garden of lush grass, cypress trees and quiet pools.

Agra, India

Petra, Jordan

Along the age-old Arabian trade routes of the mid-east was the hidden city of Petra. Founded more than 2,000 years ago by the Nabataeans at the crossroads of caravan trade routes linking Egypt, Arabia and Mesopotamia, Petra was nearly unknown to the outside world until 1812.

After going through a narrow passageway of deep canyons you suddenly come upon an ancient world of carved buildings, royal tombs and temples, chiseled from sheer sandstone cliffs and of immense size.

As shown above, a first glimpse of Petra as seen through the only canyon access to the city.

Around the world

Katmandu, Nepal
Buddhist Monk Spinning Prayer Wheels

Serengeti Plain, Tanzania

Located in Africa, the Serengeti Plain is host to one of nature's most impressive spectacles as more than two million wildebeests, zebras and a host of other animals gather on the Serengeti to calve and begin their annual 500-mile seasonal migration north in search of new grazing lands.

Around the world

Rainbow on the Serengeti

Lion Family with Cubs

Timbuktu, Mali

Founded in the 11th century, Timbuktu, located in the African country of Mali, became a major center for gold and salt caravans as well as an important center of Islamic learning. Surrounded by thousands of miles of the endless sand and barren wastelands of the Sahara Desert, this distant outpost has come to represent the ultimate in hard-to-reach places.

Timbuktu is as remote today as it was in its glory days of the 16th century. The nomadic Tuaregs, known as the "blue men of the desert" because of their traditional indigo clothing, still guide camels across the lonely dunes.

Around the World

Timbuktu Merchant

279

Timbuktu Mosque

Marrakech, Morocco

Located in an oasis of palm and olive groves, steeped in colorful Berber traditions, Marrakech is one of North Africa's most fascinating cities, the fabled gateway to the Sahara. The city is a vast jumble of mystic winding streets and colorful souks. The Place Djemaa el Fna, one of the city's major squares, is replete with snake charmers, as shown above, acrobats, magicians and other exotic performers.

Around the world

Walker Evans and Documentary Photography

One of the inspirations for my photography, dating from years ago, was an awareness of the photography done by Walker Evans and Dorothea Lange during the Depression years of the 1930s, when they worked for Roy Stryker of the Farm Security Administration.

In the summer of 1936 Walker Evans and the writer James Agee set out to photograph and write for the Farm Security Administration an article about white rural poverty in the Deep South. After several futile attempts they came across three tenant-farm families in the Hale County, Greensboro, Alabama, Courthouse square. From this chance encounter came the classic documentary photography by Evans and the writings of Agee, which eventually became the book entitled *Let Us Now Praise Famous Men.*

Evans' photographs were placed in the front of the book, preceding the title page. They were without captions. Evans maintained that the truest form of documentary photography was to record, often straight on, exactly what the camera saw. Although Evans photographed elsewhere, both before and after this era, it was the photographs taken at that time that became his greatest achievement and the period for which he is best known.

When Agee wrote his book, he used fictitious names for people and places. This was unfortunate for those coming after, who have tried to reconstruct data from his book. Even many of those writing after Agee, followed his example by refusing to use correct names and geographic locations for the three white tenant-farm families. Walker Evans did use the correct family names and locations. Only because of this was it possible for me to locate some of what Evans photographed.*

Evans, along with Dorothea Lange, recorded the seemingly plain, inconsequential details of everyday urban and rural life. They established a distinctly American style, far different from that of photographers then in the major cities. It is interesting that the one form of photography Evans never did was scenic or wildlife photography. He simply had no interest in those subjects.

Documentary photography as interpreted by Evans, was the ability to see plain everyday things as art and to record them as they are. While documentary photography can take many forms, the decade of the 1930s was the classic age of the art. Both Evans and Dorothea Lang, were expert pioneers in this area of photography, and remain so today.

In my photography, I have tried to capture what in Evans's words, "our present time will look like to those living after us." In an ironic footnote, which has nothing to do with my photography, he and I attended, decades apart, The Mercersburg Academy, which proudly possesses a portfolio of his work.

*A book which follows the next generation of these three tenant farm families (still using fictitious names for persons and places) and the rise and fall of cotton in the South, is *And Their Children After Them* by Dale Maharidge and Michael Williamson, published in 1989 by Pantheon Books, a division of Random House, Inc.

Below are the three photographs for which Evans is perhaps best known. These three people were from the Burroughs family, one of those families written about by Agee in his book *Let Us Now Praise Famous Men*. Each is shown with his or her grave marker which is located in the Oak Hill Cemetery in Moundville, Alabama. Without Evans' recording of their correct names, their identity would have been forever lost, and I would not have been able to locate their cemetery burial places.

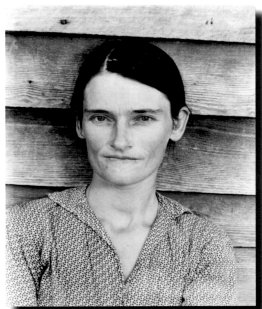

Allie Mae Burroughs
Nov. 19, 1907 – Jan. 26, 1979
age 71

Mary (Maggie) Lucile Burroughs Freeman
(Daughter of Allie Mae & Floyd Burroughs)

Feb. 2, 1926 – Feb. 21, 1971 age 45

Floyd Burroughs
Sept.11, 1904 – Dec. 27, 1959
age 55

On the following pages I have reproduced some of Evans's pictures, which I was able to obtain from the Library of Congress. I obtained those for which I was able to locate the exact place at which Evans took his pictures. I have compared his with the ones I took from the same spot decades later. It was an interesting challenge to find the places where Evans had stood seventy-five years ago. Of course it was possible to locate only a very few of the buildings that Evans had photographed and none of the people. The most permanent and least changed structures were the churches.

Sprott General Store

This general store is typical of crossroads country stores. It was photographed in 1936 by Walker Evans. The photo of the same store today shows it much changed. It is no longer a post office. *(Walker Evans above, Contemporary right)*

Sprott, Alabama

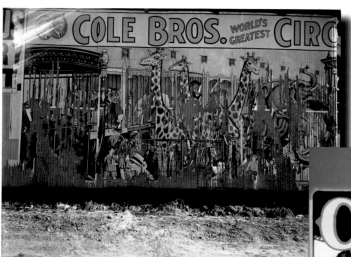

Cole Bros. Circus Billboards

Photo of Cole Bros. Circus billboards taken by Walker Evans in 1936 and the circus billboard photographed more than seventy years later, in 2009, the 125th year of Cole Bros. Circus. *(Walker Evans left, Contemporary below)*

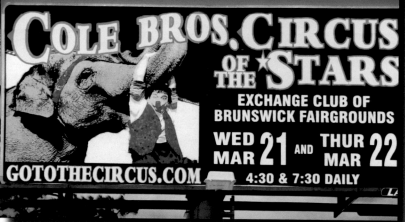

Sugar Mill Tabby Ruins

These tabby ruins are the largest in southern Georgia. Tabby is a substance made of oyster shells, lime, sand and water. It was developed in colonial times and is still used extensively in the south. This sugar mill was built in 1825 for grinding, boiling and processing of sugar cane. The size of these ruins makes this an impressive site. They were photographed in 1936 by Walker Evans, who recorded them as the ruins of a "supposed Spanish Mission" until later historical research showed them to be that of the McIntosh Sugar Mill. *(Walker Evans top, Contemporary bottom)*

Spur Route 40, near Crooked River State Park, St. Marys, Georgia

Midway Congregational Church

This church was organized in 1754 by descendants of an English colony who first came to Massachusetts in 1630, later moving south. In 1778, during the Revolutionary War, the British burned the church. In 1792, it was rebuilt on the same site. An adjacent brick-walled cemetery dates back to the same era. *(Walker Evans above, Contemporary left)*

Midway, Georgia

Our Lady Star of the Sea Chapel

Built in the early 1800s, this chapel was originally a bank, but was acquired by the Catholic Church in 1847. Walker Evans photographed this church during his 1936 visit to the area. *(Walker Evans above, Contemporary right)*

Corner of Osburne and Bryant Streets, St. Marys, Georgia

Town Square, Mt. Pleasant, Pennsylvania

More than seventy years later, this memorial stands in the center of Mt. Pleasant. *(Walker Evans above, Contemporary right)*

The state highway through the town is still Route 31

A Personal Perspective of History

There are no great men.
Just great challenges which ordinary men,
out of necessity, are forced by circumstances to meet.

- Admiral William F. "Bull" Halsey

Through the research and travel I have done to compile my three photographic books, I've developed a perspective and sense of history which has been included in my previous books. With additional time and travel, I include another essay to share with you. All of us play a part of the history during the time in which we live.

It is imperative that every civilization that wishes to survive must pass on to each succeeding generation its basic values. If any culture wishes to prevail, its citizens need to have an understanding of their own history and what has made them unique, and why their way of life is worth preserving.

Willa Cather once wrote that exposure to the best in history and literature, especially when one is at a young and impressionable age, sometimes provides "those anchors of character," which "in some unaccountable and very personal way gives us courage" and a sense of adventure and purpose in life.

great leaders are among us today. Those we now call great leaders were seldom recognized in their own time. Great leaders have become great because of circumstances which enabled them to respond to some crisis in history.

Great leaders are not usually those who seek to unify, but rather those who seek change. If we yearn for a leader to unify us, we often yearn for mediocrity. Great presidents, because they initiated new programs, were dividers, not unifiers. Certainly Lincoln was not a unifier, nor was Franklin or Teddy Roosevelt, nor Truman, not even Ronald Reagan. Truman unilaterally changed America's course in foreign policy and set the stage for the Cold War. Yet it took fifty years, many of them filled with angry controversy and danger, to win that War and to recognize Truman's accomplishments. With the passage of time and an end to the political feuding of an era, a more complete and rational understanding of American history is available to us.

Too often we in America have little desire to educate our citizens in a basic understanding of the historic struggles experienced by the pioneers, the Founders, and those who followed after them. To succeed, our culture needs to provide an appreciation of our democratic ideas as well as of those basic struggles and the contributions made by all of Western civilization.

Sometimes we wonder why all the great leaders seem to have lived in the past. However,

Yet Truman, Eisenhower, Reagan, and nearly every other leader we now consider great, lived their time under the public impression of being less than qualified. Almost all of our leaders are disparaged while in office. Consider that the British so lacked recognition of Churchill's greatness that they turned him out of office even before the war in the Pacific Theater of World War II was concluded!

Without the tyrants of Lenin, Stalin and Hitler, who created the crisis which almost drove Western civilization over a cliff where

A Personal Perspective of History

it might have perished, and resulted in World War II, there would never have been an opportunity for Winston Churchill or Franklin Roosevelt to rise to the pinnacles of leadership. It all depended on the happenstance of where they found themselves in the time of history and the events that had preceded them. Had Roosevelt not chosen Harry Truman as Vice-President, Truman would today be a little known former Missouri Senator. Without World War II Dwight Eisenhower would have never been elected President.

Consider the fact that had the French and Indian War not preceded the Revolution, or had King George not taxed the colonies as he did, the War for Independence would have taken place at another time in history, a time when the Founders had long passed from the scene. That would have changed our nation in unknowable ways.

If the Founders had been able to deal successfully with the question of slavery, there never would have been a President Lincoln. Or even with slavery, had the Missouri Compromise not been repealed, Lincoln would not have been stirred by his passions to return to politics and would have died a prosperous and yet insignificant prairie lawyer.

Without the election of Lincoln, the south might not have seceded from the Union, perhaps averting the Civil War while slavery might well have died a natural death as it did in so much of the world in the decades that followed our Civil War. Thus without Jim Crowism, there would not have been a Martin Luther King, Jr. Great crises produce great leaders.

While we tend to think that there was unanimity among the Founders, there wasn't. While they were men of great talent, leisure and education, they were also often abrasive egotists, obsessed with their own ideas. That they accomplished what they did is due more to the times in which they lived than to their individual talents.

Consider that as vice-president Aaron Burr killed Alexander Hamilton in a duel. Or that Andrew Jackson lived with bullet fragments lodged about his body as a result of wounds from duels in his own defense as well as those he fought in behalf of his beloved wife Rachel. And we decry today's partisan politics!

"We often fail to remember that nearly all the Founders were exceedingly unhappy with the changes and the direction of the government which they themselves had crafted."

We often fail to remember that nearly all of the Founders were exceedingly unhappy with the changes and the direction of the government which they themselves had crafted. Gouverneur Morris, author of the Constitution, felt that the whole document was a failure and should be rewritten. Events did not take the course the Founders had envisioned.

The Constitution that emerged from the closed-door sessions of the Continental Congress in Philadelphia, and adopted unanimously by many slave-holding, all-white males, was not at all what James Madison wanted. Yet he is often called the father of the Constitution. We seldom comprehend the partisan disputes between the Founders.

While there were sometimes bitter divisions between the Founders themselves, there were at least no national parties to carry those differences across partisan political parties and special interest groups to fan the flames of partisanship as we have today.

We salute Jefferson for his Declaration of Independence, yet how many of us have ever read that Declaration that we praise so highly? It is fewer than three pages. Really! Few recognize the name of Gouverneur Morris, perhaps our most significant writer, for he wrote the Constitution, the one document upon which every word our government looks to for definition, in only fourteen pages! The Bill of Rights was written by Madison in four pages.

And the Gettysburg Address? We're told that Lincoln put those 272 words, written in a

290

36-hour period, on the back of an envelope. Yet today's Supreme Court rulings, with nine Justices writing their opinions, may encompass hundreds of pages. For us it seems nothing is simple. And we wonder why nothing gets done.

When we were at the Founding, there were no precedents to restrain us, and no political parties to exert their partisan passions. There was no experience in the form of self government with which to guide the Founders. Too often we seem not to comprehend that we can never again duplicate the extraordinary generation of the Founders. The simple answer is that with the growth of what we today value most in America, the democracy the Founders gave us, they brought into government the participation of the common citizen which soon overwhelmed the aristocracy of the Founders closed society which the revolutionary leaders had valued so much.

> *"We've seen that the discontent and adversity between today's leaders is not much more that a re-read of the past."*

Rather than understand the facts of history we often seek to alter those facts to suit today's political correctness. We fail to recognize that a politically incorrect society could produce the genius of our way of life. Just as political machines and the smoke-filled back rooms of political bosses gave us at least as good national candidates as we have found by choosing presidential nominees in open primaries where a lifetime can be spent doing little more than raising money, traveling the country, building political IOUs and bending to every special interest group or public opinion poll has seldom given us better candidates than those hand-picked by political bosses.

Underlying every culture and civilization in history has been some form of religious God to sustain and explain its core beliefs. Man has always reached for a higher moral authority. There has always been recognition of a God, since if there is no higher moral authority than man, then it follows that moral law is whatever those in power decree it to be,

whether they are Hitler, Stalin, Gandhi or Mother Theresa. To ban the recognition of God in the public forum, so long as there is no coercion to follow that God, is not what this Republic was founded upon.

Politics in the United States in the past forty years has taken a decided turn. In the 1940s, '50s and early '60s the media tended to buttress faith in America's government and its leaders, Roosevelt, Truman and Eisenhower. However, present journalists, and too often some political leaders, seem to believe that they have a duty to undermine such faith.

One wonders where the patriotism of past wars has gone. Partisan political differences in the past stopped at America's coastline. Certainly terrorism is no less a threat than what much of the world experienced in World War II.

Too often, some Americans seem to decry the accomplishments and successes that America, with our unique form of government, has given the world. We've made this country the place to which most peoples of the world wish to emigrate and absorb our language and culture even while keeping ties to their former land.

After signing the Consitution, Ben Franklin, in response to the question, "What form of government have you given us?" answered, "A republic, *if* you can keep it." Later, knowing how politicians attempt to gain votes by promising ever increased entitlements, he perceptively wrote that, "When the people find that they can vote themselves money, that will herald the end of the republic."

As our democracy matures it seems that ever increasing numbers of our citizens seem to be willing to curtail their own freedom and responsibilities by ceding over those powers to a strong central government, all done in the name of security and entitlements, which encroach on individual freedom, opportunities and responsibility. How this plays out will be determined by future generations.

Afterward

*M*y documentary books of photographs were inspired by the photographic work accomplished by Walker Evans in the 1930s and by Ken Scott's beautiful 1988 book of photographs, *Michigan's Leelanau County* for which I have my wife to thank.

From those inspirations I began a somewhat similar book on Clearfield County. It quickly outgrew my original intention and became *Future Passages*, which included a view of a portion of central Pennsylvania. *Americana Roads*, which provides a tour of the continental United States was a natural follow-up. Most, but not all of the photographs in my three books were taken from 1986 to the present. Much enjoyable historical research, map reading and planning precedes each of our trips.

As we travel the United States, we plan each trip by the day. If the weather is not conducive to the pictures we want, we just have to take the best pictures we can and move on to the next area. There is no time to retrace our steps unless we plan to visit that same area another year.

Each generation proceeds through its own time to write its history for the next generation. No generation has the luxury of reading its history. But thanks to the history provided in written documents and photographs we can enjoy and appreciate the invitation to view the past. Our parents lived during a time which we can never fully appreciate, just as we are living through a time in which those coming after us, our children and especially our grandchildren, will never be able fully to understand.

Acknowledgments

The Dark Room
St. Simons Island, Georgia

William W. Betts, III, for copyediting the manuscript

Murphy/Carpenter
State College, Pennsylvania

Jostens
State College, Pennsylvania

And most especially to my wife Marilyn who enjoyed the
travel, including those trips remote enough to require a
four-wheel drive vehicle, and tolerated the extensive research,
planning and writing that a book of this nature requires.

This book was composed in Adobe InDesign CS2 for Windows
XP. The typefaces used on the cover and in the main body of
the book are P 22 Cezanne, Aachen, and ITC Stone Serif. The
dust jacket is 100# Lustro Dull text which has been laminated
to protect this book for years of enjoyment. The pages are
printed on 100# Lustro Gloss Text, chosen for its weight,
glossy finish, and brilliant white color. The design, layout, and
production of this book was done by Murphy/Carpenter, State
College, Pennsylvania. The images were scanned and color
corrected by PixelClear, Inc., Bellefonte Pennsylvania and
ColorTech, Lebanon, Inc., Pennsylvania, to match the original
photographs. The printing was by Jostens Commercial
Printing and Publishing, State College, Pennsylvania.